D1084901

PROUST
and his world

WILLIAM SANSOM

PROUST

and his world

THAMES AND HUDSON
LONDON

For Ruth

Quotations from *Remembrance of Things Past* by Marcel Proust, translated by C. K. Scott Moncrieff, are by kind permission of Mr George
Scott Moncrieff and Chatto & Windus. Quotations from the *Letters
of Marcel Proust*, translated by Mina Curtiss, are by kind permission of
the translator and Chatto & Windus. Quotations from *Marcel Proust:
A Biography*, volume I, by George D. Painter, are by kind permission
of the author and Chatto & Windus.

Printed in Great Britain by
Jarrold and Sons Ltd, Norwich
ISBN 0 500 13044 2

IN THE MIDDLE is my beginning and my end – or so it might be said of Marcel Proust, whose end was to preserve his beginnings, and whom it is best first to observe in the middle years of his lifetime, at the age of thirty-nine, well embarked in his famous cork-lined room above the Boulevard Haussmann on the long and great novel by which he is most known, *A la recherche du temps perdu*, translated into English as *Remembrance of Things Past*.

The theme of the book is a recapturing of his youth and the past, the writing of the book took him to a few hours before the end of his life, when, very ill and still correcting his manuscript, he sank like a captain on the bridge of his great ship – only in Proust's case he was lying down and the ship never sank but like an airship rose to the heavens to sail on benevolent wind-currents of high posterity.

A big book, and in essence a lifetime's work, for most of his previous writings and thought were directed towards it. In itself, it is one million and a quarter words long, equivalent to thirteen present-day novels of average length. Added to this must be the four hundred thousand words of *Jean Santeuil*, a first false attempt at the subject made some years previously, and finally abandoned unfinished. Added also must be essences from his first book published, *Les Plaisirs et les jours*, when he was twenty-five, and from many *feuilletons* and essays written throughout his life, even going back to his schoolday writings. So there we have up to three million words, which may again be multiplied by an immense volume of corrections and rewriting, leaving a grand total of heaven knows what, but certainly enough to make most writers pale, though none in fact so pale as he, because, as we know, he was ill most of his life.

Entrance to the Parc Monceau, where Proust sometimes played as a boy.

5

The main illness was asthma, mysterious and psychosomatic, brought on both by conscious dusts from outside and by subconscious guilts and desires from within, both a cruel cross and a blessed agent of isolation. One of the hurdles of any writer is to be master as well as slave. The master must see to it that the slave is relieved of the social pressures of people; in this the excuse of illness can help. Proust suffered from asthma, intermittently but always worsening, from the age of nine. He who loved flowers and their evocative scents was forbidden them; from each mid-April the danger of dry dust, pollen, horse-hair bedevilled the following warm months with hay fever. The bad old joke that for a man of short breath Proust's work was strangely long-winded does not accord with medical fact. The aetiology of asthma shows a marked retention of breath, a spasm closing the outward breathing function: so in fact he was in the position of one who has taken a long breath and must, at all costs, get it out of himself. Those costs, and the precautions to be able to pay them, were great indeed.

His Boulevard Haussmann apartment, part of a then quite modern building, was illy situated for a sufferer from asthma and insomnia, being both at tree-level and well within the sound of traffic along the boulevard. If you measure up the length of a horse and carriage, you will see it is all very much larger than the largest modern motor-car. And noisy with it: there was still the cracking of whips, clatter of hooves, shouting of wine-filled drivers and creaking of dray-wheels, along with the new motor sounds – Arnold Bennett six years before, in 1904, could write in the Luxembourg Gardens of 'the distant roar of traffic'. Thus, for reasons of dust, pollen and noise, Proust's windows had always to be kept closed. In addition, he had recently acquired the sound-proofing of cork-lined walls; this cork, erected on battens, was pretty thick, for when, after the Kaiser's War, he had to move, it was sold to a bottle-top manufacturer for cutting up into corks. Moreover, the curtains were kept drawn, for he slept during most of the day; and there was usually a fire in the hearth.

He lived thus in conditions of prodigious fug, exacerbated by the burning of Legras Powder inhalant for direct relief of asthma. There was also the smoke of anti-asthma cigarettes; and probably a light exhalation from some of the many medicines he took at various times of his life, trional, philogyne, veronal, dial, opium, adrenalin, caffeine, morphine, evatmïne, cola and others. Add the remains of food and drink, and the chamber-pot, and one has the whole sense-picture of those perpetually stuffy and smelly rooms of chronic invalids of the past, lairs indeed and very different from today's clean and air-blown empyrea. No flowers, of course. Manuscript and medicines mixed on the bedside-table. Certain eccentricities – for instance, a big silver chandelier kept on the floor. No counter-active perfume –

'Monsieur is afraid of the scent of princesses,' his servant was once to say to noble visitors unpermitted. (In one solidly built apartment, he was to perceive scent used by a friend several partitions away.) So, tucked away in all this, in a night-shirt swathed with woollen jackets, we find the ailing, sweating, coughing dynamo himself.

Proust at thirty-nine years old was not, naturally, like the celebrated and orchidaceous portrait of the twenty-year-old dandy by Jacques-Emile Blanche. In fact, that portrait was probably of ideal moments only; the sketch for it showed a hunched and unkempt young man, and in any case Proust was the kind of dandy who chooses his clothes with affection but soon forgets them, soon soils his gloves and lets his trousers bag; the opposite to a narcissistic automaton, he was too interested in everything to worry much about his own appearance. He could, for instance, arrive at a dinner with white tie and a mistaken morning coat. And so we have a man with ruffled hair and a thick black walrus moustache – of a kind we give to comedians today – and

The Boulevard des Italiens, by Camille Pissarro (1897).

Informally trousered Proust (left) at Trouville.

a dead white complexion, alternatively described by contemporaries as looking like a Persian prince, a walking corpse, a frightening night-owl. Owl, because the predominant feature was found in his extra-ordinarily round and intense black eyes. These, so large, showed white between the bottom of the iris and the lower lid, giving a circular and hypnotic effect, accentuated by dark lashes, by circles of heavy shadowing beneath and by black brows above of the kind which try to meet. Thus an intense circular effect, often giving people the impression that he was staring at them without seeing them at all; giving, in fact, the uneasy sensation of being watched by an animal – cat or owl – which stares and at the same time digests you inwardly.

Otherwise, his jaw was dominant, pointed to an oval yet large and strong: in some photographs it smiles in a prognathous way, the lower teeth evident as if savouring a meal. The whole face made a fine oval distinctly crowned by the charcoal curves of black hair, and in its whiteness and its pensive melancholy might suggest a moustached

Two comic drawings by Proust, sent to Reynaldo Hahn.
(*Left*) Coat of arms subscribed: 'Offert par Monsieur Castelhahn au marquis du Aan'. (*Right*) *The Trinity adored by all the saints*, after Dürer.

pierrot. Witnesses differ as to his height: his military service checks him at five feet six inches; thus presumably of nearly 'average' height, a procrustean quality which can be viewed by short people as tall and vice versa, and in any case can be greatly altered by heeled boots. An emphatic nose, giving him, as his mouth slacked open with interest, a slightly adenoidal look. Short-necked, with a large round head. With all this, a personal magnetism, an inner beauty matched by a generally handsome exterior, and the blessing and cultivation of good, considerate manners. He was soft-spoken; though quickly excitable to laughter, and at times to tears. Along with a profundity of philosophic and aesthetic feeling, he had, as is very evident in the novel, a great sense of fun.

The world of letters is not made up exclusively of those who only sigh with spaniel eyes for Art with a capital A. There is many a pocket of wit, flagrant facetiousness and high frivolity. Proust shared in all these moods. The humour in his work reflects varying degrees of comedy from a subtle wit to the broadest farce. Too many now know the happy-ish photograph of him playing tennis-racquet-guitar (lute, or by then, perhaps, banjo) on bended knee to a regally poised Jeanne Pouquet: fun, giddying at the time, scarcely repeatable afterwards. Similarly, he and a circle of friends used nicknames for each other and invented words of a private language: thus Reynaldo Hahn was Buribuls, Fénelon an anagrammatic Nonelef, the Bibescos a giggle of Ocsebibs.

9

Passing gaieties; otherwise, of course, he was deeply serious and profoundly sensitive to the material and mental scene before him. His writings have been described as having a microscopic attitude; he preferred the word 'telescopic', which is in fact nearer to his un/disguised function as a *voyeur*, with so much seen from a viewpoint of privacy framed by house windows or the windows of carriages, horse, iron/horse and motor. His first view of love is framed by pink haw/thorns, his views of trees and towers and time and his views of the social scene in restaurants or theatres or *salons* or streets seem always to be seen through intense binoculars formed by the bony sockets of his own travelling, poised skull. But these became, of course, the bino/culars of memory: enclosed in his lonely, much/peopled room, the writer naturally has to write from memory, and in Proust's case, claustrated and fumigated, writing about memory from memory, there was always an added dimension; and the reader of the novel in English may even sense a further curious dimension – the translation is so firm and secure that he may almost feel the narrator of so many French happenings to be really an Englishman disguised as a French observer. The shambling figure of Proust the author in his dark fur coat worn summer and winter can assume in the mind's eye a tartan cape, an oblique deerstalker.

Was this man so attracted by the phenomenon of high society a snob, or was he a spy of dedicated genius? It is a perpetually put question. It does not often occur to his critics that one can be both: humanity likes things tied up in precise parcels, but life itself is not so neat as that. Snobbery in any case is a big bad word covering a host of differently involved emotions: it can occur as easily among the lowest

(*Left*) James McNeill Whistler's portrait of Thomas Carlyle, which hung in Proust's bedroom. (*Right*) Sketch of the same picture by Proust, with the words: 'KARLILCH PAR WISTHLERCH'.

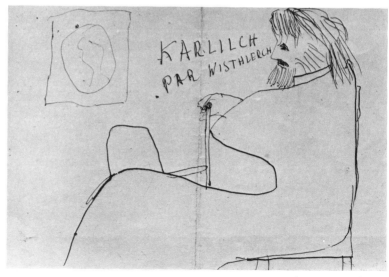

Théâtre du Vaudeville, Grands Boulevards, by Jean Béraud (1889).

'classes' as the highest, and among sportsmen and sports as in-
tellectuals and artists, and it often is simply a means to an end, a simple
erection of barriers the better to concentrate on the matter in hand –
the sport, the *salon*, the art – with the confusions of other worlds cut
out. Proust himself analyses the various snobberies of Society and the
middle classes. He sees emotional prejudice as easily at servant level as
at bourgeois level or on the true-blue heights of princely anti-
Semitism. In the novel, he pirouettes, but he records too. In his own
life, well off and brought up in a smart central part of Paris among
people on Society's fringe, he preferred aesthetically precious or orderly
groups to the other way of art, the nonconforming garret, the Bohemian
boue. (It is notable that his acquaintanceship moved in the direction of
Gide and Cocteau, rather than in the rough-and-tough of, say,
Breton or, earlier, Toulouse-Lautrec; the canvas of both his real and

his imagined life, which seems in its immensity to cover all Parisian life, really excludes much; just as he falls into the usual trap of the liberal rich, who think they know the 'working' classes by contact with a few servants, waiters, shopkeepers, fishermen, and know absolutely nothing of the greater core of grey factory-workers, black miners, mudded peasants.) But he may have sought aristocratic circles more in search of glamour and refinement than snobbish satisfaction: at least, whatever dislike he shows for others is on account of their stupidity rather than their station. He seems sometimes to have embodied the aphorism which describes an aristocrat as a man who has no need to bother about being a gentleman. Also, to a pampered well-off young man, it was all more clean and comfortable, *pace* the scent of princesses.

Later on in life, he was able to confirm his personal attitude towards snobbery in a letter to Mme Sert, wife of the painter José-María Sert, written in 1921 or 1922:

Madame,
. . . Even the sentence 'Are you a snob?' which seemed to me very stupid the first time, may now become dear to me because I heard you speak it. In itself it makes no sense; if among the very few friends who from force of habit continue to come and ask for news of me, an occasional duke or a prince comes and goes, he is amply counterbalanced by other friends, one of whom is a *valet de chambre*, another a chauffeur, and whom I treat with more consideration. Besides, one is as good as the other. *Valets de chambre* are better informed than dukes and speak a prettier French, but they are more punctilious about etiquette and less simple, more sensitive. All in all, they are worth it. The chauffeur has more distinction.

Sunday Promenade at Saint-Cloud, by Henri Evenepoel (1899).

Portrait of Misia Sert by Auguste Renoir. She was one of the leading figures in the intellectual and artistic world of Proust's Paris.

In his youthful tendency towards the aristocratic world, Proust was not unusual: the artist at court is familiar throughout history, and today, in many capital cities, there is usually a coterie of first-rate writers and painters who live it up with the nobs, as distinct from their equally talented fellows who find a greater reality as far as possible away from them. But although it was natural enough for Proust to take the high way, there was a further and more complicated motive: predominantly in his character he was the excluded man, and exclusive areas plainly beckon the excluded. He was excluded from various sectors of life as an invalid, as a Jew, and as a homosexual. He was excluded by a bourgeois background, and by having an imaginative nature with its complementary longing to be accepted into the easier-looking life of philistine 'bloods' (cf. in the novel, the narrator's ambitions towards the sporting 'frieze of girls' playing along the front at the seaside). He was excluded very early in life by the birth of a younger brother, who stole his mother's attention; he was excluded, as a child more sensitive than most, by the sound of grown-ups enjoying life at night when he must stay lonely in bed. He feared to be excluded, and thus invited exclusion, in love affairs early and late; so that, at least in his relations with women, he chose to fall in love with the impossible – with women far older than he, or with women socially too high for him, or with a courtesan unacceptable in Society; and when none of these was available, then most particularly did he search out women promised or married to friends of his and thus politely proscribed. Excluded, he both fortified his exclusion and sought to break it down. With his homosexual loves, he preferred in the end the employed secretary, the physically captive love whom he kept materially secure on the excluded premises. Again, he welcomed social ostracism in some circles as a Dreyfusard, not only as a loyal Jew and a humane liberal, but as a victim of anti-Semitism. Finally, in the pleasure-pain of all this, he felt very deeply the exclusion of the past, his expulsion from the remembered paradise of childhood.

By the autumn of 1910 he engineered a further expulsion, he made almost absolute his lifelong tendency to sleep during the day and to rise to work, and sometimes to go out, during the night. All these kinds of exclusion infer the deeply apprehensive sense of it, not necessarily the real closed door. Proust, in fact, penetrated many doors. Society received him, at a time when new Jewish blood was becoming generally acceptable on condition of some extra expertise, like wit or money; though one must remember that he was only half-Jewish, was brought up as a Roman Catholic, and had at the time that romantic Persian or palely princely Arabian appearance, which must have stood him in good fashionable stead when *Schéhérazade* and the Ballets Russes struck Paris in 1909. What is impossible to assess is the influence of his mother; how much she was a usual type of dominant mother over-worried by her son's sickness, and how much might have been added to this by the tribal strength of what is known loosely today as the beloved 'yiddishe momma'. (There is a curious echo of Proust in the anglicized Armenian Michael Arlen, whose work created hero-circles of blond, upper-class, white-tied Mayfair men-about-town of the twenties, a mythically enchanted lot who tended finally to dissolve in a Proustian disenchantment of chivalrous disease and brave rot: Arlen was also nominally excluded, willingly accepted.)

Proust had always been both a blessing and a nuisance to his friends and loves. He was entertaining, a brilliant talker, and – always a good party trick – an accomplished mimic. He was also touchily sensitive and emotionally possessive. When he sensed the cold shoulder, he went after it at high temperature indeed; the excluded are quick to advance. However, one blessed element in his character seems to have been a complete lack of malice. In a society where wit and actions of a malicious nature were quite commonplace, something considerate and compassionate and honest in his nature precluded him from enjoying the easy vice of malevolent action. He could, if irritated, reply

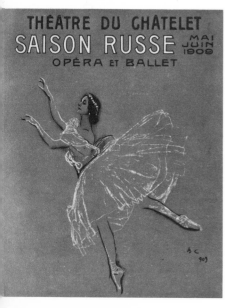

Poster announcing the first season of the Ballets Russes in Paris, 1909.

with a cold and intelligent irony. But no more than that. Perhaps, being a man of perception, he recognized the cheapness and ease of malice; or perhaps he simply was not tempted, never even thought of it. In any case, of this he seems to have been quite innocent. If at times he may sound cruel or heartless, this would not have been from a wish to hurt but only from a desire to reach some general truth.

He has been accused of obsequiousness: one may not be sure of this, flattering behaviour is difficult to separate from normal French manners of the time, from the 'cher maître' quality investing literary circles, from the purple delight of a writer over-decorating his written correspondence. But certainly he was profuse. And capped it all with a typically Proustian duality – he was generous and thoughtful to a high degree, yet could suddenly be the most inconsiderate of men.

A great social event in 1904. The Comtesse Greffulhe leaving the Madeleine on the arm of the Duc de Gramont on the occasion of her daughter Elaine's marriage to the Duc de Guiche. The Duc de Gramont was the bridegroom's father; both he and the Comtesse suggested characters in Proust's novel.

Before Proust was born – the sort of
scene he wished he had experienced.
In 1867, when the character Charles
Swann was in his heyday: *Official
Celebration at the Tuileries during the
Universal Exhibition of 1867*,
watercolour by Henri Charles
Antoine Baron.

Thus, he would unbelievably expect his friends to conform to his own
noctambulist hours: he would call on people long after midnight
(often in search of information, the meaning of a phrase, the explanation of some social mannerism), and would issue an invitation for, say,
six in the morning, when the fortunate friend might be expected to
view the carving of the portal of Notre-Dame (where Proust was in
fact seen once at dawn, his fur coat thrown over a night-shirt). The
duality meets in his treatment of servants who chauffeured, took
dictation or kept house for him. He paid them much more than was
normally necessary, he expected from them absolute silence during the
day and prodigies of attention at night and at dawn; errands, *pneus*,
refreshment must be attended to without delay – reasonable in those
days of master and bell, but gruelling at such normally unreasonable
hours. To serve Proust was a specialist's job. Though in manner he
was no tyrant, being always most consciously polite: for instance, there
is recorded an occasion when he addressed a note to a friend's porter in
the following capacious terms, 'Monsieur le Concierge de Monsieur
le Duc de Guiche'. And why did he overpay, over-tip? To make
sure of acceptance? To make sure of comfort? It also smells of the
arriviste: but that does not quite hold water, since it was also the

attitude of the superlative Parisian gentleman to disregard money, to scatter it casually; in this Proust was perhaps in the end a little old-fashioned, behaving more in the manner of a man of the Second Empire sixties, when the snobbism of squandering reached phenomenal heights. Though certainly, he was reproved for overdoing things by aristocratic friends.

Without doubt he was physically brave, if also physically petulant. In younger years, he had fought a duel with pistols. And even in middle years he was still quick to suggest a duel when affronted in public – though still more worried by the time of the duel, at a dawn hour when he was usually considering going to bed, than by the danger of wounding or death. Duels by then, of course, had become fairly safe: it was the accepted course to fire wide with the pistols, though with swords some blood must still be let. Nevertheless, weapons are sharp and human temper can be sharper; there was always the danger of an opponent being either eccentric or losing his temper, and the memory of the Mores–Mayer Affair, when Captain Armand Mayer was killed, died hard. The white-faced Proust seemed not to care; very different was his attitude to discomfort or any circumstance that might accentuate his illness – he would dine out at the most formal table in his overcoat, he would write long letters to his hostess about the temperature of the room and the necessity for windows to be closed. A visitor to his own rooms might have to suffer him conversing only by written notes, so as not to disturb his inhalation; and woe betide the neighbour who employed workmen on some hammering alterations – all work might have to be relegated to the afternoon. It is forgivable, both asthma and insomnia are complaints of an exhausting nature. And both militated against his immensely assiduous devotion to work. How often he brought them upon himself is another matter.

A revolving pistol presented by Proust to the Duc de Guiche and Elaine Greffulhe as a wedding gift. The case was decorated by Frédéric (Coco) de Madrazo, and inscribed with verses by Elaine when a child.

The changing Paris of his time presents a particular Proustian
appeal. The opening volumes of the novel are placed in his childhood
and in the years before he was born, years which his parents knew and
which are perpetually attractive, forever just unattainable to an
envious child.

His own childhood was spent in the decade after the Commune;
but the love-affair of the mysteriously attractive grown-up family
friend Swann took place in the gilded heyday of the Second Empire.
Thus, Swann can be connoted with the crinoline; Proust's puberty
with the bustle. To spot a crinolined Boudin and talk of Proust's seaside visits to Cabourg is inaccurate. Just as it is inaccurate to place
the *salons* of the Faubourg Saint-Germain necessarily in old mansions
on the Left Bank; the Faubourg at the turn of the century had become
less a geographical than a social entity and had mostly moved to
smart new areas on the Right Bank. And the new boulevards and
streets of the Right Bank were then a lot more modern than we, if we
are occasional visitors, usually feel.

Throughout his life, apart from an infancy at Auteuil, Proust always lived in a small smart area round about the Saint-Augustin Church and the Parc Monceau. First the Boulevard Malesherbes and the rue de Courcelles in his parents' lifetime, then for many years the Boulevard Haussmann, before a removal to Réjane's house for a few months, and afterwards the final eyrie on the fifth floor of the rue Hamelin. It was thus a part of Paris largely rebuilt after the great eruption of Baron Haussmann and his new boulevards in the fifties and sixties. Transferred into today's terms, Proust lived as it might be in a large luxurious concrete and glass apartment put up before the Second World War, still newish in feeling and with no romance of the past. The endless lines of white grey-mansarded seven-storey houses were elegant but not of much character, unprepossessing except where here and there a touch of stone vermicelli announced *le style moderne*. If Proust uses the word 'modern' as applied to architecture or objects, it will usually be to this form of Art Nouveau that he refers. Green-painted Art Nouveau grilles distinguished the entrances of the

Wide-lensed perspective showing the Church of Saint-Augustin. The Proust family lived in the Boulevard Malesherbes to the left of the church. To the right, the Pépinière Barracks (where, one night in the nineties, the adult and wild Duc de Mouchy danced naked in front of the troops).

19

Place de l'Europe on a Rainy Day, by
Gustave Caillebotte (1877), showing
streets near the Gare Saint-Lazare,
the railway station which Proust used
for his visits to Normandy and to
reach Mme Aubernon's house near
Louveciennes.

Métro stations, the first line of which opened in 1900. The end of the
century saw the retreat of Fabergé before the whiplash of Lalique and
Tiffany. The first public telephone boxes had been at work since
1885, the special smell of those old vulcanite receivers was an established part of sensory life. France, not yet America, led Europe in
automobile and aeronautical matters (witness the survival of words
like chauffeur, garage, aileron, etc.): the turn of the century saw the
golden years of brass-twinkling, leather-smelling De Dion-Boutons
and Delaunay-Bellevilles, whose odour of petrol could speak to
Proust not of polluted air but of days out in the country. Similarly, he
is most conscious of the first aeroplanes, going so far as to liken the
movement of Giotto's angels at Padua to aircraft imminent upon
loops of the loop. Proust lived through a mighty street revolution
from horse-drawn victorias and landaus to the electric coupé and the
petrol-driven landaulette. In most ways, modern inventions then

(*Above*) Operators at a Paris
telephone exchange *c.* 1890. Proust
was much intrigued by their voices,
and wrote of them as, for one
instance, '. . . the umbrageous
priestesses of the Invisible, the Young
Ladies of the Telephone.' (*The
Guermantes Way* I). (*Left*) Art
Nouveau motif on a Métro staircase.
Hector Guimard designed most of
these stations.

touched everyday life more than they do today. The radio and tele-
vision and some medicines number among the very few new factors
which really touch our lives: astronautical programmes and the
computer remain distant mysteries. We are more affected by the
development of earlier inventions: flying as a common means of
transport, the massing of the motor-car, the development of the supermarket. But in Proust's lifetime there arrived like a bomb a kind of
supermarket in department stores like the Bon Marché: life was peren-
nially astonishing. And remarkably confused – Proust had an
electric hotpoint in his bedroom, from which he could draw a
description of milk boiling over on to books and papers, while a
multitude of Parisian houses had never even had gas-light, but still
used oil and even candles.

Nothing could have looked more grotesquely and unromantically
futuristic than the giant iron taper of the Eiffel Tower; yet this was
opened in 1889 for the centenary of the Revolution, with a tricolour
searchlight fanning the now Republican skies. By 1900 balloonists
were using wireless telegraphy, the cakewalk had arrived at the Jardin
de Paris, the explosion of anarchist bombs had given way to a new
frisson, the knife of the wickedly popular *apache*. Paris streamed now
with bicyclists; the elderly elegant Prince de Sagan had helped
popularize cycling in the Bois, Edmond de Goncourt records seeing

The Eiffel Tower, constructed for the
1889 Exhibition.

Luxury lighting in 1895: the last
stand of oil against electricity.

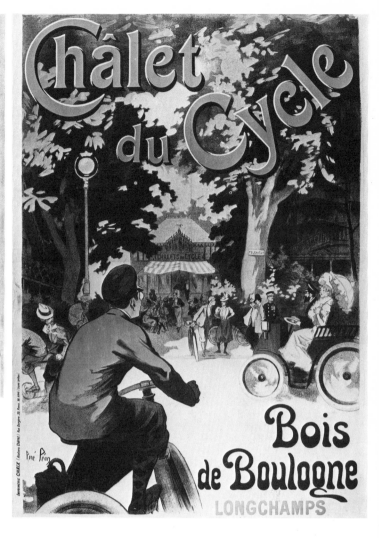

Bloomers and knickerbockers adrift
in the Bois de Boulogne.

'fat little Zola' pedalling along with his mistress, and Arnold Bennett
records a strangely quiet night-time Champs-Elysées sporting the
solitary Chinese lantern of a bloomered lady-cyclist. The invention of
the elevator and the increase of traffic quite suddenly made the cheap
top floors of houses the most expensive. It was indeed a time of
startling change, much of which Proust was faithfully to record along
with his larger picture of the decline of an exclusive aristocratic
Society, that nodding but tenacious old brontosaurus which finally
went under with the coming of war.

New blood was coming in; men of noble line like Boni de Castellane
went in search of American heiresses, jewel-squandering Russian
dukes were two a penny at Maxim's, the industrialist and the Jew
were accepted more and more into the drawing-rooms of the great.

23

La Place du Trocadéro by Ernest Renoux, showing the Mozarabic Trocadéro across the Seine as seen through the benevolent arch of the Eiffel Tower. With a motor car and park chairs, we have a Proustian view of new and old.

Next door to Proust's favourite *fin de siècle* café, Weber's, there was an 'Irish' bar. But Paris of the Parisian, with its rich Napoleonic legacies and its magnets of Art and Fashion, was still the queen-bee city of Europe, the *ville lumière* where everything that was anything went on.

To such musics of change, the claustrated Proust laboured on, as ready to appreciate the enormity of a Mozarabic Trocadéro as the smell of petrol, as prompt to rhapsodize for two pages on an ice-cream as to immortalize the hawthorns of his childhood holidays at Illiers or show us the final fountain of a grand, expiring *salon*. By 1912 he had ready the first volumes of his novel: they were published in November

An electric automobile in 1899, a
sign of the times.

1913, to the appreciation of a considerable few, but not the really large
readership he had hoped for. The outbreak of war prevented publication of the next volume: throughout the following long years he
worked steadily expanding and rewriting what he had written,
bringing the *Götterdämmerung* of Society up to date, and introducing
the war itself, going even so far as to remove his childhood Combray-
Illiers piecemeal from the plains of Chartres to the eastern front line,
so that it could be occupied by Germans – until the present enormous
work of genius was almost completed at his death in 1922. Un-
willingly, he profited from the war; and so has posterity.

25

Soldiers fire on the Communards'
barricades near the Panthéon, in
1871. The Panthéon is the flag-flying
domed building on the centre left.

(*Right*) The Auteuil railway station
after bombardment. Abnormal then,
this kind of chaos is thought to have
affected Proust and his mother, who
was then bearing him. The family
had moved from central Paris to
Auteuil to avoid such danger.

How, now, did this strange tenacious figure with the fluffy moustache come about? Back to the beginning, to a moment in the womb when his father, apprehensive of the fighting of the Commune in 1871, removed his pregnant wife to her uncle Louis Weil's engardened villa at Auteuil, a suburb at the further end of the newly laid-out Bois de Boulogne, where, on 10 July 1871, Marcel Proust saw the first nerve-racking light of day.

His father was Doctor, later Professor, Adrien Proust, a physician who became eminent as an authority on the control of epidemics by means of the *cordon sanitaire*. His mother was a cultured and beautiful Jewess, Jeanne Weil, whose father was a well-off stockbroker.

The young Marcel turned out to be a thin and sickly child, and this was attributed to the stresses of the fighting and the scarcity of proper food consequent upon the Prussian siege and its bloody aftermath. Two years later his brother Robert was born, strong and healthy – but to the toddling Marcel a far stronger peril than the previous lack of diet. To Marcel's credit, he suppressed his jealousy of his brother throughout his life – there were probably compensating protective impulses at work, too – and they remained loving friends always: any

Professor Adrien Proust, Marcel Proust's father . . . and Marcel's mother, looking here more Neapolitan than Jewish, more *mamma* than *momma*.

27

Robert (*left*) and Marcel (*right*) Proust.

frustrations were removed into an oedipal sphere, but here again the young Oedipus seems to have suffered a curious setback, for it is well recorded in the opening chapters of the novel (probably closely autobiographical) that at a moment of crisis, lonely for his mother's love, it was the big competitive father-figure who proved suddenly kind and understanding, instructing the mother to spend the rest of the night with him. Here was the never-to-be-forgotten scene of the missing good-night kiss, when his mother remained downstairs with guests and the lonely loving boy upstairs grew nearly hysterical in his left-out misery. Henceforth, his deepest passions were to be turned towards his mother, he had learned the first lesson of emotional blackmail: a fit of histrionics had ended not in punishment but in high victory. That night, in the novel, his mother reads to him from George Sand's *François le champi*. (It happens to be the story of a young man who eventually marries his foster-mother: to a child's ears, the 'foster' is quickly elided.) Now the great love-hate wrangle was begun. It is symbolized by the withheld good-night kiss, but one may feel that it is really more the adumbration of all the long lonely hours of early bedtime on summer nights, when a sensitive or precocious child

(*Opposite*) *A Corner of an Apartment*, by Claude Monet (1875). At the same period, the young Marcel Proust was spending much time thus luxuriously alone.

The asymmetrical church tower at Illiers. Of the similar tower in the fictional town of Combray, the narrator's grandmother lovingly said: 'My dears, laugh at me if you like. . . . If it could play the piano, I am sure it would really *play*.' (*Swann's Way* I)

hears the sounds of grown-up laughter and enjoyment, and longs and longs to be up too: he is the only one in the world left out, and as he listens in bed or through the banister railing he yearns most deeply for the time he can stay up all night. In *Les Plaisirs et les jours*, a much earlier writing, Proust describes just such a little boy of seven's feelings when he listened to his mother dressing for a ball – and begged her to leave early 'because he could not endure the idea that, while he was trying to sleep, anyone was preparing for a party, preparing to go out'. Mark that 'anyone'; not necessarily the mother. It is precocious envy of a lasting kind. It is the moment when a child swears that when he grows up *he* will stay up all night. Which might also, if felt deeply enough, well lead to a lifetime's induced insomnia.

The garden bell at Great-Uncle Louis's house no longer rings – the construction of the Avenue Mozart silenced it long ago. But it is perpetuated in the fictional bell of Combray, just as whispered references to an unknown, enticingly gilded 'lady in pink' (probably

The market-place at Illiers.

Laure Hayman, his great-uncle's mistress) fascinated, by the grown-ups' bated breaths, his child's ear. It was at Auteuil, too, on a later family visit when he was nine, that during a walk in the Bois he suffered his first and terrifying attack of asthma. Under the trees, among the beloved flowers heavy with poisonous pollen; and perhaps at a moment of nervous distress in the company of his family. From then on he was not only a delicate child but a child with a specific and frightening affliction.

When his doctor-father Adrien Proust could manage to leave Paris, the family spent holidays at the house of Jules Amiot, Marcel's uncle by marriage, at 4 rue du Saint-Esprit in Illiers, a market-town of grey sandstone near the wide Beauce plain south-west of Chartres. Illiers had been a stopping-place for pilgrims from Paris to Santiago de Compostela, and the now-celebrated madeleine cakes with their scalloped shell-shape were moulded after the shells which, plentiful on the Galician beaches, the pilgrims picked up and wore in their hats.

Illiers offered more than madeleines to the young Marcel – it gave him his paradisal view of the countryside of virgin youth, of again a garden, and of the two famous family walks, the way of Méréglise with its hawthorns (Méséglise of the novel) and the watery way on the banks of the Loir towards Saint-Eman (Guermantes). Charles Swann's enchanted garden of Tansonville is a reflection of Uncle Jules's separate pleasure-garden on the outskirts of Illiers, a garden called the Pré Catelan, echoing the meadow in the Bois named after the murdered medieval troubadour Catelan. The two ways, real in childhood, became symbolic – Swann's Méséglise way the way of love and affirmative joy; the Guermantes way, with its naiad mystery and the more secret shadowed life of violets and water-lilies, was the way of Merovingian romance and sophisticated dreams of Society.

His Aunt Elisabeth was an invalid who lived apart in her upstairs room, and, ironically, for she was of his father's extrovert stock, gave the young Marcel his first picture of the trappings of hypochondria, of the sanctity of voluntary seclusion. In her room with its lemonwood furniture there was a bedside chest of drawers on which were mixed medicines and religious books – an admixture which Proust in the novel records as 'both pharmacy and altar . . . to keep the proper times

Uncle Jules Amiot's pleasure garden, called the 'Pré Catelan', at Illiers – possibly the prototype of the fictitious Charles Swann's garden at Tansonville.

Garden view of the Amiot
household at Illiers. Proust's
bedroom window is on the left.

for pepsin and for vespers' and which in his own later life he was to
reproduce in a bedside table of medicines and manuscript. Aunt
Elisabeth was also always on the watch through her window, and
would have taught the boy, along with the magical essences of lime
tea and madeleine, his first lessons in calculated observation. Life in a
town like Illiers was then, and to a lesser extent still is, ruled, or at
least inhibited, by the unseen eye. Unlike, say, an Italian town, where
life is lived on the streets, the country towns of northerly France have a
deserted and puritanical air, a sense of daily thrift behind closed doors,
yet laced eyes at every window. Those people on the streets were there
for a purpose: for an errand, for shopping, or they were workmen in
their ubiquitous blue smocks. All these were noted by the eye at the
window; as also any stranger, even the phenomenon of a strange dog,
whose appearance would stimulate feverish inquiries from the
cloistered invalid. Downstairs lay another enclave of childhood

wonder, Ernestine's kitchen, a place to love and linger in, as with many children in those homelier days – a place of exciting pans and smells, vegetables and life, and at times of rarer excitations, such as the phenomenally priapic raw asparagus, whitely thick and at one end pinkishly mauve as a glans, and invested with the mysterious power, after digestion and micturition, of 'transforming my humble chamber into a bower of aromatic perfume'.

Pink was the colour of paradise, the pink of hawthorns, the mystery of grown-up love's lady-in-pink, the pinkish freckles on the face of the little girl Gilberte seen through the hawthorns, even the pink of the strawberries and cream cheese mixed 'with the experience of a colonist' by his Uncle Jules. Yet the pink was already flawed by

Little Girl with a Watering-Can, by Auguste Renoir (1876), recalls Proust's vision of Gilberte at Tansonville.

(*Opposite*) Another view of the Amiot garden at Illiers. Proust's garden in the imagined Combray had similarities, like a lilac tree, like 'neglected soil'.

(*Above*) *Plage à Trouville*, by Claude
Monet, in the 1870s.

(*Right*) *Le Déjeuner*, by Claude
Monet (*c.* 1873).

Henriette in the Big Hat, by Henri Evenepoel (1899). She suggests something of the probable mischief of Marie Bénardaky, the girl with whom Proust played in the gardens of the Champs-Elysées.

growing pains, by the cook Ernestine who taught him his first lessons in human cruelty, the vicious slaughter of chickens and the mental torture of housemaids; interrupted, too, by growing intellectual pleasures, as with the Abbé who awoke his first interest in the etymology and magic of place-names. And soon, as he grew older and holidays began on the sea-coast of Normandy, he found that the garden of childhood and Illiers was already part of the past.

Yet one last garden remained, that of the Champs-Elysées, where from the Malesherbes residence he was taken to play, and where he met the delightful Marie Bénardaky with whom he fell in boyhood love and whose dear, unattainable presence is now enshrined in the character of the novelist's second vision of a growing Gilberte Swann.

Proust (top right) at the Lycée Condorcet (*c.* 1887) which he left in 1888.

(*Below*) *The Exit of the Lycée Condorcet*, by Jean Béraud (1903).

Proust was now a day-school boy at the Lycée Condorcet, and when we read his finely remembered perception of this period of the world still young and with virgin mysteries excitedly at hand, the phrase 'your schooldays are the happiest of your life' does not sound after all so silly, for they are not only the last years free from adult responsibility but as well an arbour of last innocence and the final years of true discovery. After then, everything is at second-hand, re-experienced. Nevertheless, such paradises can be found again: not in material reality, as when Proust's return to his lily-strewn childhood river discovered only a disappointing muddy stream, but in the other reality, that existing forever in the isinglass of memory and best retrieved not by conscious thought but by a chance passage of the senses, taste, smell, touch, sound, angles of light once seen long ago and never forgotten – realities that have never truly ceased to exist at all.

At the Lycée he came in time to the philosophical and metaphysical teaching of an intelligent and well-liked master, M.-A. Darlu. To find such a sympathetic and beneficent instructor is one of the most fortunate chances that can come to any young man. Darlu's influence is traceable in the very essence of the great novel. At the same time he had as fellow pupils Daniel Halévy and Jacques Bizet, who inspired

and edited schoolboy magazines in which Proust wrote in one essay of moonlight seen from his Boulevard Malesherbes window, expressing thus so early some of the essential magic of *A la recherche* in miniature. In this piece, he first sees himself at the age of fifteen bored in his bedroom by the ordinariness of things, the dull play of the lamp, the clatter of crockery from an adjoining room, the dark night sky. As George Painter in his biography of Proust writes: 'Then he is seventeen, it is the present, and everything is transformed: the Boulevard Malesherbes below his window, with "the blue moonbeams dripping from the chestnut trees", and the "fresh, chill breathing of all these sleeping things", becomes a night-scene as exquisite as the moonlit garden of Combray, and "usual things" are no longer horrible. "I have made them sacred, and Nature too, because I could not conquer them. I have clothed them with my soul, with the inner splendour of images."'

What else would he have seen in those days? What would have been some of the usual elements of the Paris street scene calculated not to dull but brighten a boy's eye? As we know from the novel he went with much excitement to the domed advertisement columns, bright kiosks displaying the latest theatrical posters – perhaps at the time

'Every morning I would hasten to the Moriss column to see what new plays it announced.' (*Swann's Way* I)

(Opposite) *L'Arc de Triomphe*, by Giuseppe De Nittis, showing one of the ways to get to the Bois de Boulogne and the fashionable Allée des Acacias, where *les grandes horizontales* vertically sauntered and, particularly in the person of Léonie Closmesnil, gave Proust a conception of the courtesan-character he called Odette de Crécy.

(Opposite below) A portrait of Mme Emile Straus, by Elie Delaunay (1878). One of Proust's first hostesses, she remained a lifelong friend.

designed by Toulouse-Lautrec or Mucha. Then also a number of *carrefours* were brightened by the new Wallace fountains, whose watery jets played silver against a background of cream or grey façades. If the young Marcel were taken to play in the Parc Monceau, he would have passed horse-buses, and soldiers with blue coats and red trousers, and in the park itself the little brown iron chairs still to be found everywhere in French parks today. And if in the early eighties he had been taken above the park to the Boulevard de Courcelles, he might have seen lowering across the roofs a giant figure, a huge spike-crowned lady holding a lamp – the Statue of Liberty being prepared by the sculptor Bartholdi before its shipment to New York. The sunsets then would have seemed especially magical, with wonderful streaks of green among the lurid reds and golds – the dust from the eruption of the volcano on the East Indian island of Krakatoa affected the European upper atmosphere for three years after 1883. A few doors away from his parents' home stood the grand mansion of the Comte and Comtesse de Maillé at No. 3 Boulevard Malesherbes, and this is likely to have inspired the narrator's proximity to the Guermantes Paris residence. Apart from the Champs-Elysées gardens and the

The Statue of Liberty, destined for New York Harbour, under construction in Frédéric Bartholdi's yard behind the Boulevard de Courcelles (1883).

Parc Monceau, his walks took him to the Bois de Boulogne and its fashionable parade called the Allée des Acacias. Here in the elegant crowd he noticed particularly the figure of Léonie Closmesnil, a celebrated courtesan, driving in her carriage or strolling on foot; and so was born a first image of the novel's Odette de Crécy.

Two of his fellow pupils, Baignères and again Bizet, happened to be the sons of two important well-to-do hostesses, and by 1888, when he was seventeen, he was introduced to their *salons*. Mme Straus, widow of the composer Bizet, was later to become a lifelong friend. The Guermantes way was begun.

Such is some of the backbone; the flesh was weaker and often wounded – Daniel Halévy recalled later that 'there was something about him which we found unpleasant . . . poor, unhappy boy, we were beastly to him'. The young Marcel, in fact, was too profuse with his emotions, which were misunderstood as melodramatic, obsequious, hypocritical. At the same time, with both his apparent delight in the social *levée* and the gushing prose of too precious writing, he founded his reputation as an idler of the *salons* and a dilettante of the pen. This etiolated mud was to stick for many years.

(*Left*) Anatole France, etched by
Edgar Chahine. France was the first
established author Proust met, thus
suggesting his writer-character
Bergotte.

(*Right*) *Henri Bergson*, by Jacques-
Emile Blanche. Bergson, professor of
the duration of Time, instructed
Proust at the Sorbonne.

At eighteen, at Mme Arman de Caillavet's, he met Anatole
France and in him the beginnings of his writer-character Bergotte:
France was physically disappointing, an example of life not living up
to its imagined expectations, and echoing a favourite theme that to
travel is better than to arrive. In this *salon* Proust also met Mme Arman's
son Gaston, who was doing his military service at the time. Proust was
attracted by his tales of barracks-life, and also attracted by the imminence of a new law abolishing the voluntary military service of one
year (if you could afford uniform and maintenance) and making the
period of enlistment as long as a compulsory three years. Before the
old law ran out, then, he joined the infantry at Orléans. Thus the
beginnings of the soldiering character Saint-Loup and the barracks
at Doncières, and for Proust himself a strangely enjoyable year in
uniform for a young man of so unmilitary a nature.

It is sometimes thought that the company of other young men
excited his so far latent homosexual leaning. What might have
been far stronger was the sudden relief of acceptance, unquestioned
acceptance, in an area where he might have expected ridicule or
aversion: instead, class prejudices were disarmed, intellectual pre-
tensions sunk, and there came good comradeship on a 'we're all in the
same boat' basis – it is a relief familiar to many who have joined the
services expecting trouble and finding the opposite. He was, too,
lucky in his officers, who were paternal and understanding. He could
write afterwards of a happy time '. . . in which pleasure is the more
constantly with us because we have no time to run about looking for
it and so miss it altogether . . .' He even asked, unsuccessfully, to stay

Proust in the infantry at Orléans. This monkish pleasantry is inscribed to Gaston Arman de Caillavet.

on for a further few months. When later he was questioned as to what event in military history he most admired, he answered with ambiguous humour: 'My own enlistment as a volunteer.' Alas, Trooper Proust passed out only as the penultimate number of a large class of some sixty odd.

And passed on to the Sorbonne and Bergson. The duration rather than the apparent stop-go of Time was Henri Bergson's subject, as it was also to be Proust's, when finally a chance experience of involuntary memory proved to him Time's true durational entity. Theory entices, practice realizes: in his correspondence and other writings Proust does not stress any influence of Bergson on his own theories; but this proves little, a writer is often quiet about such sources of influence, or is even unconscious of them. However, it may be pertinent that a book of Bergson's, published in 1896, *Matière et mémoire*, considers in detail the problems of aphasia in its bearing on memory and the continuity of durational time: was it a coincidence that much later in life Proust became an intermittent aphasiac? Had something stuck, a Bergsonian memory, beyond the momentary faculty of speech?

A view of Cabourg-sur-Mer
(*c.* 1900). Cabourg, and its *plage*,
played its part in Proust's fictional
Balbec.

(*Opposite*) Pink and blue pastel by
Julius L. Stewart (1882) of Laure
Hayman, Proust's blueprint for his
fictional 'lady-in-pink'.

Jeanne Pouquet, the girl on the chair in that tennis photograph, was
the fiancée of Gaston Arman. Probably partly because she was thus
honourably barred, Proust fell for her: nothing more than the nourish-
ment of yearning came from this, together with a further facet of the
character Gilberte. At these tennis afternoons at Neuilly he never
played, but sat on the fringe among the girls' 'gossip corner'. There was
nothing necessarily effeminate in this: many a creative observer cannot
abide games, the abstract concentration on the flight of a little ball, but
instead prefers the scene, the gaiety, the voices, the other play of light
and summer shade. It was this same group which asked him to fill, in
an amateur theatrical piece, the part of Pierrot: he would have been
exact with his pale oval face and large dark eyes. And with his
mooning, susceptible, tenacious heart.

In this same 1891, his twentieth year, there was a further holiday at
Cabourg and Trouville, when Blanche sketched him for the celebrated portrait with the orchid. In the winter he met again Laure
Hayman, his great-uncle's cocotte love, the lady-in-pink and print in
blue for Odette. This 'educator of dukes' had an intellectual grace,
collected Saxe figurines, and aptly described a pleased young Proust
as 'my little porcelain psychologist'. Here too is a clue that his attitude
in the social round was not all honey-sucking, he was observing and
questioning and coming away with pollen on his feet, raw material
which was later to bear fruit, fused and fixed by memory. It was
sometimes thought that his friendship with Laure Hayman was more
than platonic – it is a long time ago, and that essential phrase in

(*Left*) Various voyeurs at the Opéra in a painting by Henri Gervex exhibited in 1880. This was 'the Guermantes way'.

(*Right*) *The Comtesse Greffulhe*, by Philip A. de László de Lombos (fashionable portrait-painter known commonly as 'Laszlo') (1909). The Comtesse was considered to be the most beautiful woman of the Parisian Upper Crust of those days. She was Franco-Belgian-blooded, with chestnut hair, black eyes with yellow lights – and part-precursor of Proust's Guermantes ladies.

consideration of other people's sexual lives, even contemporary, must be rigorously applied: 'I was not there.' Nevertheless, the chess-game of jealousy and romance was certainly in full play – Proust flirting his attentions between Jeanne Pouquet, Laure Hayman and the brilliant, unassailably virtuous figure of Mme Straus. He was also flirting with the printed word, his first published pieces occurring in a small magazine *Le Banquet* (The Symposium) in 1892. There was a sketch of Mme de Chevigné, placing her in white in a box at the Opéra just as the Duchesse de Guermantes appeared many years later in a famous passage of the novel. He fell in love with the eagle-faced Chevigné, at a distance, lingering in the street, longing, finally rebuked.

It was in Mme Straus's drawing-room that he met the Comtesses Chevigné and Greffulhe, precursors of the Guermantes ladies, and the elegant Charles Haas, friend of Edward VII and of the exiled pretender to the French throne, the Comte de Paris. Haas was a man of Jewish blood yet a member of exclusive clubs, welcomed there for his culture, his charm, his bravery in the Franco-Prussian War. Here – and Proust is still only twenty-one – enters the main figuration of Charles Swann; in company with shades of the quizzical and ironic

46

Emile Straus, and of the dramatist Hervieu whose upturned moustaches had 'tiny icicles at the corners'. Among this moneyed jet-set of the period, Proust met in the various *salons* a few writers like Jules Renard, and painters like Forain: and now, in 1892, a further dimension of the human animal strides on to the scene of fruitful memory – the heavily powdered, dyed-haired, portly, staring-eyed figure of the homosexual Baron Doasan whom Proust first saw at Mme Aubernon's house in the rue d'Astorg. Doasan's appearance and manner fit exactly the first appearance of the Baron de Charlus to the narrator by the theatre poster at Balbec; an author will retain such a first visual conception long after he has introduced different and foreign characteristics into this personage whose physical presence remains unaltered on the screen of the mind. The other main prototype of Charlus, Montesquiou, was more so in character and manner than in appearance, for Montesquiou's physique was thin and angular, 'a greyhound in an overcoat', as he described himself.

At Trouville in 1892 Proust met Marie Finaly of the sea-green eyes, fell romantically in love, and for once this love, in an innocent youthful manner, was returned. 'J'aime de vos longs yeux la lumière verdâtre' – the Baudelairean phrase hummed among the great trees

A garden scene, showing Charles Haas to the extreme left. Haas was the prototype of Proust's Charles Swann. Mme Straus sits centrally, with Degas in painterly profile behind her (*c.* 1888).

(*Above*) Madeleine Lemaire, hostess and painter of roses, in her studio in the rue de Monceau, near the Parc Monceau.

(*Left*) Medallion of the green-eyed Marie Finaly after her marriage. She was probably the most successfully romantic female love of Proust in his early twenties.

The poet and eccentric *poseur* Comte Robert de Montesquiou outside the vestibular rotunda of his home, Le Pavillon des Muses, in the Boulevard Maillot, *c.* 1904. He was part-prototype of the Baron de Charlus.

and the long carriage drives on the way to Honfleur, and the phantom of Albertine of the novel was raised in a brief summer's love. Marie Finaly was his last young lady-love for many years; in the same way, the sterile yearning for Mme de Chevigné put an end to a succession of incestuous dreams of middle-aged mother figures. Now he began a series of deeply emotional, but platonic, friendships with young men.

In the following spring he met the redoubtable Comte Robert de Montesquiou, then aged thirty-eight, in the studio *salon* of Mme Lemaire, painter of roses. The Comte was a nobleman of ancient lineage, and an almost acrobatic snob: he was notorious as an aesthete and poetaster, and celebrated this in the most high-flying terms: 'I have added to our ducal coronet the glorious coronal of a poet.' He was, though, a fairly incisive wit, but easily malicious. Tall, black-haired, rouged, Kaiser-moustached, he cackled and screamed in weird attitudes, giggling in high soprano, hiding his little black teeth behind an exquisitely gloved hand – the *poseur* absolute. He was said

49

to have slept with Sarah Bernhardt and vomited for a week after-wards. He was homosexual but not promiscuously so, in this parting company with the character of Charlus; he kept his affection mainly for his secretaries, like the Basque Yturri, who coincidentally was stolen from that stouter physical prototype of Charlus, Baron Doasan. Vain, insolent, dangerous, this brilliant and hollow *poseur* made his mark of terror on Society, yet also graced it as a figure of eccentric exoticism. Proust seems to have remained on guard with him, offering an adulation close to servility.

For instance, in one of many letters to Montesquiou one finds passages like this:

In lieu of your presence, which, by its lightning glance, the stormy galvanism of the voice, the precision of the silhouette, excites one even more violently to thought, I take every opportunity to consult your writings or your words, whose flame I carefully cherish in my memory and which it illuminates.

Or again:

And I believe that this is what has preserved in you this unalloyed generosity which is now so rare – as well as having permitted the most subtle of artists to write poems so powerfully thought out as to ensure for themselves an enduring place even in a very slender anthology of French philosophic poetry; which has made the sovereign of the transitory, sovereign of the eternal, as well; and which, finally, prevents our foreseeing the future course of your work, since wherever there is a spontaneous outburst, a fountain head, a true spiritual life, there is freedom. All this to the great good fortune of your respectful and grateful

Marcel Proust

It was Montesquiou who finally introduced Proust to figures in the highest echelon of Society, in 1893.

We might pause here for a moment to consider in general the enormous list of Proust's friends and their various influences on the characterization of his novel. Very many books have now been written about Proust; and in all of them, however scholarly, a certain ob-fuscation prevails, a fog legitimately made up of so many names, but giving the lay reader a dizziness familiar from the morass of names in long Russian novels, or even the Bible. Since Proust died as late as 1922, the means of documenting his acquaintanceship has been the more available; since he was a capacious letter-writer, and since, though ill, he was socially vigorous, the people of his world proliferate and become further confused by a whole different but similar world of duplicate names which peoples the novel, a macrocosm in itself. That will be why this present account quotes as few names as possible: there may still be many, but they will more stand as examples of the many, which in any case the interested reader will find well documented in such excellent biographies as George Painter's large two-volume work.

Secondly, there is the whole question of the novel as a *roman à clef*. When questioned, Proust himself emphasized that any one character was the composition of eight to ten facets of real people he knew. Any exact attempt to trace a full characterization in real terms is bound to be incomplete, particularly in that any working novelist knows that characterization comes also from chance mental photographs of people whose names he may never know or could know, the passing world of the man in the bus, the girl in the bar. Nevertheless, since Proust's real hero was his own exact and sensuous memory, and since he moved in fairly prescribed circles, the people of his novel may more than usually be found in the real world he lost and finally regained. Once, at least, in a very curious passage, he addresses almost by name one of the prototypes of a character in the novel. It occurs after the death of Charles Swann. In an extraordinary mixture of fact and fiction, he addresses the shade of a real person:

The Interior of a pâtisserie, by Jean Béraud (1889). This was at the Rond-Point des Champs-Elysées, and was the kind of place where Proust might have seen some passing and unknown girl who could later have entered his novel.

51

And yet, my dear Charles——, whom I used to know when I was still so young
and you were nearing your grave, it is because he whom you must have regarded
as a little fool has made you the hero of one of his volumes that people are beginning
to speak of you again and that your name will perhaps live. If in Tissot's picture
representing the balcony of the Rue Royale club, where you figure with Gallifet,
Edmond Polignac and Saint-Maurice, people are always drawing attention to
yourself, it is because they know that there are some traces of you in the character
of Swann.

Although not exactly named, this could only be addressed to
Charles Haas, the standing figure in the grey tall hat. At the same time,
the narrator 'Marcel' of the novel becomes for a brief moment Marcel
Proust himself; the anonymity of his carefully disposed hall of mirrors
momentarily quivers into plastic personality, he has come guardedly
clean.

To assist in part the general identification of characters, there is a
short table of prototypes among the appendices here. For the moment,
one might be content with closer visualizations of a few of the main
hostesses and noble ladies he knew. The first two give some presence
to the *arriviste* character of Mme Verdurin: they are Mme Aubernon
and Madeleine Lemaire. Mme Aubernon was already sixty-seven in
the second year of the nineties, lively and plump and loud, and 'looked
like Queen Pomaré on the lavatory seat' according to Montesquiou.
(*La reine Pomaré* was a former Tahitian queen; but also the soubriquet

of a contemporary cocotte.) Mme Aubernon's dinners were strictly regimented, with a conversational topic ordered beforehand, and she went so far as to ring a little bell to command silence for any guest who happened to be speaking. There is the well-known story of one man so silenced, who, when asked afterwards what he wished to say, had to reply: 'It's all right – I just wanted another helping of peas.' Nevertheless, there was merit among the Aubernon stringencies; they bred a hothouse flowering of wit and heightened conversation, and it was her drawing room which offered such revolutionary dramatic pleasures as the first French production of Ibsen's *The Doll's House*.

Madeleine Lemaire's was the liveliest and most crowded of the bourgeois *salons*, counting many minor artists such as the genre painter Béraud, and including many of the *gratin* who rolled up in their carriages to view, as in a zoo, such talent. The receptions took place in a large studio giving on to a small lilac-hung garden, where by day Mme Lemaire painted her popular rose pictures. She was a tall woman, wigged, well rouged, with the required energy of a great hostess. Her Tuesdays, unlike Mme Aubernon's Wednesdays, included the recital of music, with its rows of chairs, its respectful silence for the artiste. She also owned a country-house near Paris, which was reached by 'a little train', and which gave much to the conception of Mme Verdurin's ambitious villa near Balbec.

Madeleine Lemaire's country-house near Paris, the Château de Réveillon (Seine-et-Marne). From here Proust sent such postcards as this; and here he smelled the Bengal roses that reminded him of Illiers.

53

The Comtesse Adhéaume de Chevigné, photographed in 1889. Proust found her to be his blue-eyed bird of happiness for some time; and, with her aquiline nose and wit, part of his fictional Duchesse de Guermantes.

(*Below*) Batwing frock by Poiret, *c.* 1910, decorated by Mariano Fortuny, the Catalan designer who inspired dresses for Proust's fictional Albertine.

Two stars of the Faubourg Saint-Germain, elevated and exquisite middle-aged morsels of the Upper Crust, were the Comtesses Adhéaume de Chevigné and Elisabeth Greffulhe. Mme de Chevigné, a descendant of Sade, lived in the rue de Miromesnil, where each afternoon she received a regular attendance of prominent clubmen, who encircled her as she delivered from aquiline features witticisms later attributed in the novel to the Duchesse de Guermantes. She spoke in a hoarse low voice (the Dietrich, the Garbo of her day?) and smoked through a holder a chain of black tobacco cigarettes, thus dispensing the same mascara *caporal* smell which then as now distinguished the French olfactory air, along in those days with horse dung and sweat on the streets, absinthe, cigar smoke, rich scents such as patchouli and new musks from Russia. The Comtesse had brilliant blue eyes, golden hair, and bird-goddess features of beaked nose and thin predatory mouth – a lady perhaps less feminine than formidable. Her dress was particularly elegant, and it was from her that Proust seems to have gathered essentials for his captive Albertine's gowns by the Catalan designer Fortuny. Odd reminders of the falcon features echoed to Proust later in his friendship with Hélène de Chimay and the Princesse de Noailles, whom Harold Nicolson described as a hawk-goddess from an Egyptian hieroglyph.

The Comtesse Elisabeth Greffulhe was a cousin of Montesquiou, the greatest beauty of her day, and a lover of the mauve orchids which became in the novel the Swann⁄Odette love⁄call: 'Shall we do a cattleya?' Some of her characteristics go towards the Duchesse de Guermantes – her relations with her hearty husband, her cousinship with Montesquiou (as Charlus), and, for instance, the silvery laugh which Proust compared with the carillon at Bruges. Also, this chestnut⁄haired, black⁄eyed, superlative beauty contributed towards the half⁄Bavarian Princesse de Guermantes, who dressed in a similarly showy way, as we see in her appearance at the Opéra. Besides her great beauty, the Comtesse Greffulhe must also have been gifted with a generous intelligence, for she remained the constantly adored of Montesquiou, who managed to quarrel with pretty well everybody else.

Thus a taste of the *salons* and hostesses of the Parisian nineties – a *salon*, of course, meaning a drawing⁄roomful of regularly invited guests, and occurring at various times of day, as afternoon or evening receptions, or as dinners. It is notable here that still as late as 1917–18 Proust was checking up with a Society footman on various procedures of seating and invitation: although he had been through it all, he was not a natural aristocrat, and well knew that in those circles, while few eyes batted at a change of liaison, the misplacement of a stitch of

The Comtesse Anna de Noailles, a plaster bust by Rodin (*c.* 1906).

(*Below*) A room of reception in the country⁄house near Paris of the Princesse Mathilde, a niece of Napoleon I famous for her literary gatherings.

clothing, an accentuation, a gesture could send the *arriviste* immediately back down a few rungs of the ladder. Here also is an argument for the biographer who searches for real persons behind Proust's characters; in the interests of truth, he would very likely have played safe by using real specimens – though accepted, he knew he was still not of the real water, a treacherous liquid pooled with fatal dialectics of behaviour. Also, to be invited with the *gratin* did not necessarily mean meeting them; even on the premises, one had to seek a further introduction, and follow this, if granted, with some performance of wit or worth. However, Proust persisted in achieving the highest circles – though in fact such circles were not quite so rigorously exclusive as he portrays them; the Upper Crust was softening year by year.

Genre paintings of these receptions do not quite catch the tone, the painter's problem of composition isolating too comfortably the figures. The few existing photographs are truer, and the packed assembly gives a feeling more of the crush of a present-day cocktail party, though then of course smokeless and more formally dressed.

The wit of those times also sounds an echo of what one might loosely hear today. At random: of a husband's mistresses, 'the little ladies who make such good mattresses'; and, 'Everyone says you're silly, my dear, but I always tell them they exaggerate.' Such barbed delights are true of any literate period; and, of course, in print lose the importance of timing, delivery, the shockability of those present, the general intoxication of a gathering.

By his twenty-second year Proust had made his personal advances to a series of safely unattainable ladies – a top-grade courtesan, a friend's fiancée, an irreproachable bourgeois hostess, a countess of the true *gratin* – along with a few more attainable girls. Now, as he climbed the social ladder, he was also to climb away from women into the arms of men. What precisely decided this change cannot be known; possibly it was gradual, since it began with a few platonic but possessive friendships. But now the first known male lover takes the scene, Reynaldo Hahn, a nineteen-year-old composer and singer from Venezuela, pale brown, handsome, gifted, Jewish, moustached. He performed with fashionable success for Society, and occupied Proust's love-life for the next two years. How much sexual and how much romantic any such association can be is, again, only to be guessed at: intercourse can have eunuchoid or ascetic or primarily spiritual qualities – it has been said that Proust was 'virile', but only hearsay suggests this and only definitive letters would prove it. Certainly there are stories of one or two early visits to heterosexual brothels – in one case calling in bed for hot-water bottles and more bedclothes to help keep him warm; less certain are rumours, never too well proven, of his arrangements in later years for rats to be tortured in his presence, to

Reynaldo Hahn. Composer and singer from Venezuela; a love and friend of Proust.

satisfy some need for sadist-fetichist orgasm (if true, this had possibly something to do with early sexual fantasies stimulated by the slaughter of chickens at Illiers, and transposed to some Freudian revenge on mother, brother, father or authority itself). But this and his more usual sexual experiences must remain, as is their private nature, his own.

During these social years, and even to be capable of the physical demands of so many *salons*, he was not so ill as later. The asthma was intermittent, predominant as a seasonal hay fever, and there were minor rheumatic and stomach pains. At the same time, his pieces in *Le Banquet* continued to foreshadow similar passages in the later novel, and now he was also published in *La Revue blanche*. As to the Sorbonne, he obtained his degree in law in 1893, and in 1895 the degree in philosophy. In that year also his father faced him with the necessity of a career, and Proust faced his father with the necessity of a life of letters, all resulting in a sinecure at the Mazarine Library. He remained thus largely free to continue the social round, holidays in Normandy, occasional travels just beyond France, his own minor incursions into the literary world, and now a passionate entrance into the latest province of exclusion, the freemasonry of Sodom. It was in

For *La Revue blanche*, a poster by Henri de Toulouse-Lautrec (1895). Misia Sert was the model.

May 1894 that Proust attended Montesquiou's splendid fête at Versailles in particular celebration of his new pianist protégé, Léon Delafosse, and which the hard core of the most Upper Crust attended: thus Proust saw combined in one evening the public apotheosis of the Cities of the Plain and Society at its most exclusive. His directions were confirmed.

In his twenty-fifth year, family deaths came – Great-Uncle Louis Weil and Grandfather Nathé Weil died. But there was also a birth, that of his first book, called, in allusion to Hesiod's *Works and Days*, *Les Plaisirs et les jours*. By now severe asthmatic fits had returned, possibly summoned by socialite and sodomite guilts: his social dilettantism had not gone uncriticized, and at that time the public hint of homosexuality was a slur on the honour serious enough to

(*Opposite above*) Proust, back-centre, at the villa of the Princes of Brancovan near Evian-les-Bains, on the Lake of Geneva.

(*Below*) Katabexine, 'a sovereign remedy against coughs of every nature', including whooping cough and asthma.

59

An illustration from Proust's *Les Plaisirs et les jours*, by Madeleine Lemaire (1896). Proust sits third from the left. The book was spirited but precious, and decorated with flowers by Lemaire and music written by Reynaldo Hahn.

(*Below*) Lucien Daudet, taken in 1896. Son of Alphonse Daudet, and a very close friend of Proust.

merit a duel. On this score, he was indeed to fight a duel in the following February with the journalist Jean Lorrain. Lorrain, criticizing rightly the preciousness of the book with its melancholy *douceurs*, its floral decorations by Lemaire, its music by Reynaldo Hahn, and its preface by Anatole France, had wrongly added a pejorative thrust hinting at a homosexual relationship between Proust and Lucien Daudet. And here we have an arras-ful of open secrets; for Lorrain was a podgy painted pervert of the Doasan kind, which guiltily growls through its own powder at effeminacy; and Proust had indeed begun an affair with the successor to Reynaldo Hahn, Lucien Daudet, described by Jules Renard as having 'a little squeaky voice which he takes out of his waistcoat pocket'. The pistols were ritually discharged on a cold wet afternoon at Meudon. Proust's only fear had been that his morning bedtime hour might be chosen. Honour was satisfied, 'Marcel was brave, frail and charming', commented his old school-friend Robert de Flers. Nobody was hurt.

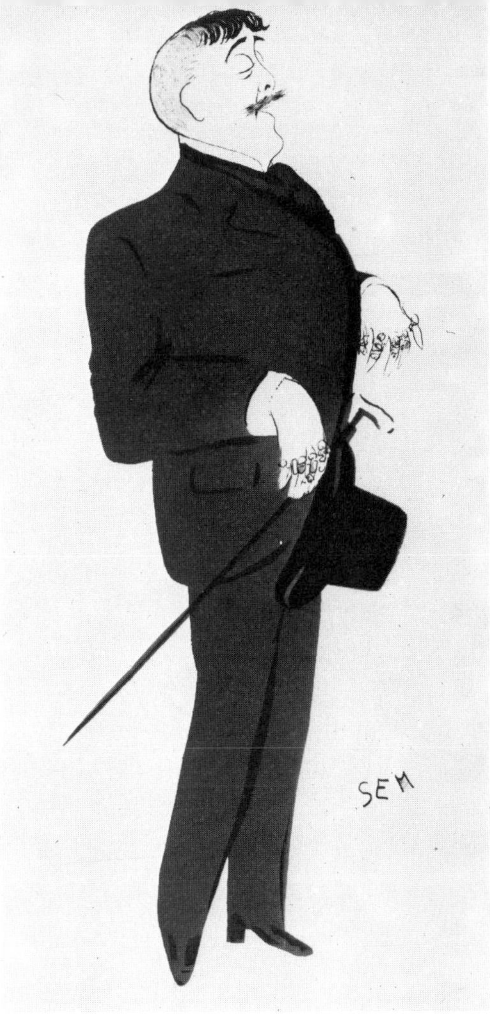

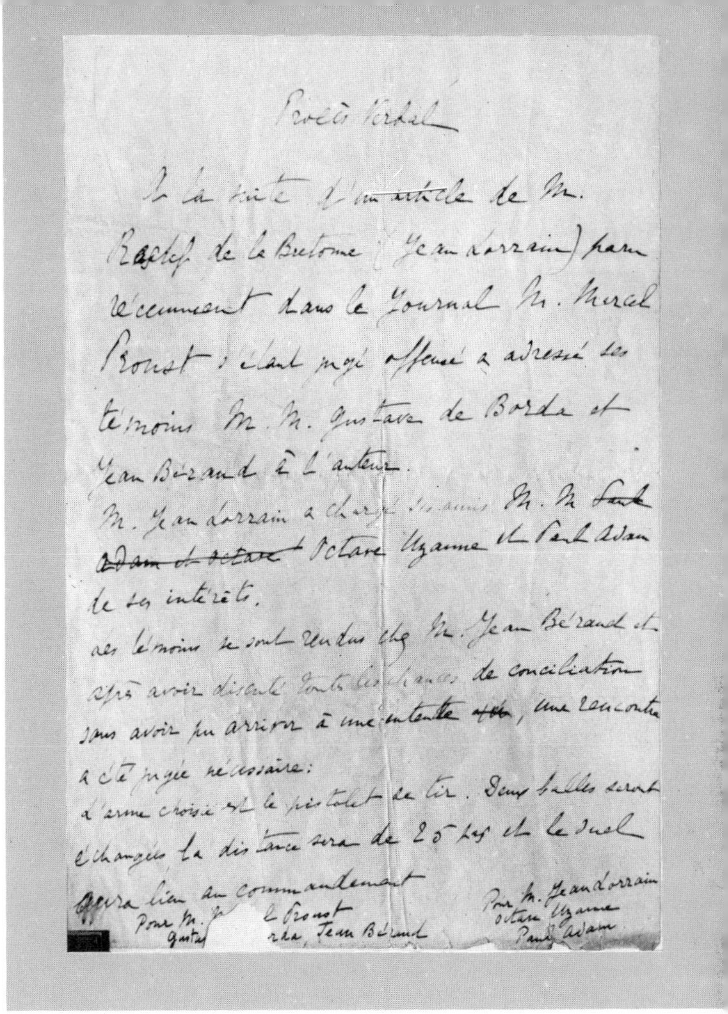

Procès Verbal

À la suite d'un article de M. Raitif de la Bretonne (Jean Lorrain) paru récemment dans le Journal M. Marcel Proust s'étant jugé offensé a adressé ses témoins M. M. Gustave de Borda et Jean Béraud à l'auteur.

M. Jean Lorrain a chargé ses amis M. M. ~~Paul Adam et Octave~~ Octave Uzanne et Paul Adam de ses intérêts.

Ces témoins se sont rendus chez M. Jean Béraud et après avoir discuté toutes les chances de conciliation sans avoir pu arriver à une entente ~~afin~~, une rencontre a été jugée nécessaire:

L'arme choisie est le pistolet de tir. Deux balles seront échangées la distance sera de 25 pas et le duel aura lieu au commandement

Pour M. M. Proust
Gustave de Borda
Jean Béraud

Pour M. Jean Lorrain
Octave Uzanne
Paul Adam

However, two years before this another and undisclosed battle was engaged – the attempt to satisfy his literary honour with a long work. *Jean Santeuil* was begun: and by September 1896 he had enough prepared to begin negotiations with a publisher. The novel has the same autobiographical element as *A la recherche*, though with different emphases: the extraction of the withheld mother's kiss, the Illiers childhood, evocations of the strawberry summer day, the chicken slaughter, schooldays – these and much more appear, together with significant manuscript errors, sometimes naming the otherwise fictitious village Illiers, sometimes writing 'I' for Jean. The thematic conception of 'the two ways' is absent, though, most importantly, Proust's obsession with the mystery of Time is deeply scored. The writing of *Jean Santeuil* continued through the latter part of the nineties, but the secret of time and memory still eluded him: and he himself began to see a sterilty in the work, whose heroic failure he finally recognized.

Jean Lorrain, cartooned by SEM. Proust fought a duel with Lorrain, in his twenty-fifth year. Lorrain seems to have some physical resemblance to the Baron de Charlus.

(*Right*) *Procès Verbal* of Proust's duel with Lorrain.

SALON DES CENT

EXPOSITION E. GRASSET

Poster for the Salon des Cent, by
Eugène Grasset (1894). This design
is much in the mood of the time.

Escape from this apparent cul-de-sac came from two disparate and
unexpected quarters – the English essayist John Ruskin and the con-
demned Captain Alfred Dreyfus. But for the time his social life
continued, along with quiescences of lonely writing and reverie.
Anyone who has had a long childhood illness knows its benevolent
by-product, the ability to watch, savour and dream alone in a bed in a
room. The external world removed, one is at the mercy of the slow
passage of dying light across a sunset wall, the figuration of friezes and
wallpapers, all the presence of time passing so very, very slowly. The
ability to muse and dream is learned forever. Adult illness is too
conscious of itself to teach this; though it can re-experience an almost
mystic elevation through memory, once there has been that all-
important seclusion in childhood. Thus the bedridden child in
Proust is reiterated throughout his tormenting, though finally
benevolent, ailment. One may even conclude that, beyond the
veneers of tragedy, his neurotic life was not too unhappy: he had the
ultimate blessing of a vocation, a creative quest he believed in and
lived with more closely than is possible with external humanity.

Extreme sensitivity works two ways; hurt is magnified but so is joy
– Proust, for instance, could say that a pansy, the only flower his
asthma allowed him to go near, 'smelled like skin'. One can go little

Sarah Bernhardt, by Manuel Orazi (*c.* 1900–3). Apart from an essay in *le style moderne*, there might be a presage of the moment of Proust's large discovery with toast and tea in 1910.

further than that. But now these subtle senses were allowed exercise only at night, thus mostly at the remove of memory, as the habit of nocturnal work and daytime sleep took a closer hold on him. At his parents' Malesherbes apartment, he spent the nights at the red-clothed oval dining-room table, by oil-light, with a fire burning well into the spring. The apartment was furnished with Second Empire cosiness and fuss, as were many of the rooms Proust visited in an era of potted palms and plush-draped easels: but at the same time the vogue for *le style moderne* had begun, and he must have seen rooms by Lambert or Majorelle, though he never seems to have made much of them; the nearest he got was the work of Emile Gallé, whose vases, though technically new, were decorated with botanical realism: Proust, while assessing the present, always preferred the past. Just as one hardly hears of him at a newly opened Maxim's, but rather at the conventionally luxurious Restaurant Larue. The climate of these years was one of great psychological change – the end of a century when some breathe relief, others expectation. It was a time as well

(*Left*) The Comte Boni de Castellane who entertained lavishly.

(*Right*) Tables laid before the Fête des Acacias, given at the Palais Rose, their home, by the Castellanes (*c.* 1896).

when inquiry into the nature of the mind's working was refreshed: Charcot's hypnotic experiments had been made, Freud was busy in Vienna, and Proust must have heard much discussion of these between his doctor-father and his surgeon-brother Robert. Something in the air indeed – and later, in the first decade of the twentieth century while Proust was at last embarked on *A la recherche*, coincidentally Alain-Fournier was writing *Le Grand Meaulnes*, many of whose scenes are suffused with the same adolescent mystery, the same yearning for lost paradise, as Proust's.

In 1897 Boni de Castellane held his memorable ball in the Bois, which cost three hundred thousand francs of his American wife's money, employing the entire *corps de ballet* of the Opéra and a multitude of flying swans released among fireworks and 80,000 Venetian lanterns. Proust was there. Proust himself entertained in these years, not of course on Boni's scale, but lavishly enough at dinner-parties at No. 9.

Like many another son of well-off parents, his personal finances see-sawed. As we have seen, he was generous and emotionally spend-thrift. Yet there were money rows with his father and mother, and we find him troubling to write to a high commissioner of the railways to obtain a ten-day extension of a return ticket from Brittany. His correspondence with his mother is strewn with references to the expenditure of quite small amounts, ten francs here, four francs there, showing that he had to be most conscientious in these minor money affairs. It was champagne one day, cider the next, a pattern he would follow for many years, long after his parents' deaths. He was apprehensive of money losses, yet would hire the whole floor of a country hotel to ensure quiet.

To the dancing boom of the *chahut* and other last light frenzies of a giddied century, the Dreyfus Affair erupted to divide a suppressedly militant France. The Captain was deported to the Guiana penal colony in 1896; the conservative military, still bristling for a Prussian revenge and instantly alerted by any smell of German intrigue, were righteously satisfied, despite such near-farcical disclosures as the official hiring of a charwoman to bring the contents of the German

The Stock Exchange, by Edgar Degas (c. 1879).

65

L'AN
FRANÇAIS ILLUSTRÉ
ORGANE DE LA LIGUE ANTISÉMITIQUE DE FRANCE
Journal Hebdomadaire

UNE BANDE D'ESCARPES

Captain Alfred Dreyfus on his way to the prison van (1894); and an anti-semitic paper showing the Lady of France protecting her country against foreign enemies. Behind her

Georges Clemenceau is prepared to stab her in the back. This was all part of the Dreyfus controversy, which changed French social conditions. Proust was a Dreyfusard.

(*Below*) Illustration by C. Léandre from *Le Rire* (1899). It shows Major C. F. (Walsin-) Esterhazy being dropped in the torrent of human *immondices* by the Hand of Justice.

LA MAIN DE LA JUSTICE JETTE ESTERHAZY DANS LE TORRENT DES IMMONDICES HUMAINES SOUS LE REGARD DU DIEU VENGEUR DES INIQUITÉS

Military Attaché's wastepaper-basket daily to the French War Office. But in November 1897 *Le Figaro* published the famous Esterhazy *bordereau*, and the whole question of a revision of the trial exploded. Zola wrote his *J'accuse*, Proust collected the first signatures to a Dreyfusard manifesto finally signed by three thousand prominent artists, writers, professors. In taking such a course, prompted by both Jewish loyalty and liberal humanity, Proust risked ostracism in many of the social circles into which he had so tenaciously clambered: the Jockey Club and much of the *gratin* were plainly anti-Dreyfusard. However, Society like society soon became split on the question, as quickly it snowballed to mountainous proportions. Finally, the whole affair lost its initial concern for the unjust fate of one unhappy captain, and became a free-for-all battleground of socialists and conservatives, Semites and anti-Semites, laity and clergy, and any other group which wished to align itself against another. The gem-like flame of *J'accuse* became a gassy flare of *Je m'excuse*, until the final reinstatement of a pardoned Dreyfus in the Army as late as 1906.

Emotionally involved, yet still able clinically to observe the acro-batics of Society on the Dreyfus score, Proust grew gradually dis-enchanted with the world of coronets: they were not, after all, worn by a race of medieval heroes of ultramarine blood, but by ordinary fallible folk rather more affected than most. He continued to know them,

Captain Alfred Dreyfus rehabilitated (1906). He was also awarded the Légion d'honneur, later served in the First World War, and achieved the rank of lieutenant-colonel. He died in Paris in 1935.

The gilded Virgin on the south porch of the Cathedral of Amiens. This sculpture partly inspired Proust in his translation of John Ruskin's *The Bible of Amiens*.

though no longer in a state of rapture: it was the embryo of all the pages of disillusion to come later in *A la recherche*. At the same time he began to cultivate new friends, like the Noailles set near Geneva, and like Reynaldo Hahn's English cousin Marie Nordlinger, who reinforced a growing interest in the ideas of Ruskin. He now turned to writing his first essay on Ruskin and his churches, and would soon begin the translation of *The Bible of Amiens*, and later of *Sesame and Lilies*. His grasp of Ruskin's mind and intentions was immediate and instinctive, despite an imperfect knowledge of English. But both Marie Nordlinger and his mother were to help him with this problem of the language.

The century was turning, the great and kindly Alphonse Daudet had died in 1897 from an early syphilis, and such a milestone seemed the more ominously significant at the time. Proust himself was iller, more reclusive – though he still stayed in great country-houses and in the 'grand' type of hotels. It has been easy and fashionable to sneer at the grand wedding-cake hotel. But to the properly creative observer the life lived therein is as valid as any other, and Proust could be exactly visionary or howlingly funny in these sophisticated and worldly circumstances. For instance, he shows in his novel that to a rich old man in search of kitchen-boys the servants' quarters became magically seductive: 'He loved moreover all the labyrinth of corridors, private offices, reception-rooms, cloakrooms, larders, galleries which composed the hotel at Balbec. With a strain of oriental atavism he loved a seraglio, and when he went out at night might be seen furtively exploring its purlieus.' And again in a brilliant passage on a hotel lift, which should be quoted in full, he describes the operator, at the pressing of a bell:

. . . rushing down towards me with the agility of a squirrel, tamed, active, caged. Then, sliding upwards again along a steel pillar, he bore me aloft in his train towards the dome of this temple of Mammon. On each floor, on either side of a narrow communicating stair, opened out fanwise a range of shadowy galleries, along one of which, carrying a bolster, a chambermaid came past. I lent to her face, which the gathering dusk made featureless, the mask of my most impassioned dreams of beauty, but read in her eyes as they turned towards me the horror of my own nonentity. Meanwhile, to dissipate, in the course of this interminable ascent, the mortal anguish which I felt in penetrating thus in silence the mystery of this chiaroscuro so devoid of poetry, lighted by a single vertical line of little windows which were those of the solitary water-closet on each landing, I addressed a few words to the young organist, artificer of my journey and my partner in captivity, who continued to manipulate the registers of his instrument and to finger the stops. I apologised for taking up so much room, for giving him so much trouble, and asked whether I was not obstructing him in the practice of an art to which, so as to flatter the performer, I did more than display curiosity, I confessed my strong attachment. But he vouchsafed no answer, whether from astonishment at my words, preoccupation with what he was doing, regard for convention, hardness of hearing, respect for holy ground, fear of danger, slowness of understanding, or by the manager's orders.

John Ruskin's pencil-and-wash impression of the Casa Contarini-Fasan in Venice (1841). In 1900 Proust, imbued with the ideas of Ruskin, visited Venice.

The year 1900 took Proust to Venice and Padua with his mother, travelling the long way via Turin, for it was still six years before the Simplon Tunnel. In the novel, such a tedious journey seems to pass like a flash, as the narrator and his mother gossip about a forthcoming marriage: it is strange that Proust, so fond of trains, strikes no major descriptive chord on this great international steam-train journey, which, swathed as he was in rugs against draughts, bedevilled with footwarmers and noises, must have inconvenienced him considerably; but perhaps he drugged heavily against these discomforts. Not so with the journeys on 'the little train', whose strongest source was the local railway at Thonon by Geneva, and whose lyrical meandering he loved and described with all the tender nostalgia the English have since learned from Sir John Betjeman.

But Venice – once there Proust delighted in this first visit to a southern and unique city. Among his brilliant descriptions, one impression remains particularly forceful. This is the immediate relationship the narrator draws between Venice and his childhood Combray. It begins on his first morning, when the shutters are thrown back to show him for the first time the dazzling power of the southern sun. His eye fixes not on the sun-blackened slates of Saint-Hilaire but on the Campanile's golden angel. 'In its dazzling glitter, which made it almost impossible to fix in space, it promised me with its out-stretched arms, for the moment, half an hour later, when I was to appear on the Piazzetta, a joy more certain than any it could ever in the past have been bidden to announce to men of goodwill.' He goes on to find echo after echo of Combray in hot sunny weather – and, looking between the lines, for it is never stated explicitly, the reader may suspect that it is all really a return to that ever-memorable sort of solid sunlight which in every man's mind distinguishes the golden age of childhood. Southern sunlight, so extremely dazzling, so still, so hot, so incapable of movement or shading, has a set permanence about it very similar to the equally permanent sunlight of memory. The days of childhood blaze in this weighted way. No cloud could obscure it. 'And as I went indoors . . . I did indeed recapture, coming from the warm air outside, that feeling of coolness that I had known long ago at Combray. . . .' Only the southern sun could thus recall the sun of a heat-wave in a northern country, and particularly the exact quality of the golden permanence of summers long lost in childhood.

The rue Royale and the Place de la Madeleine. Proust patronized the Café Weber and the Restaurant Larue on the left-hand side.

Back in Paris, there followed now the years of his patronage of the Café Weber and the Restaurant Larue in the rue Royale. Apart from literary friends he began consorting in platonic friendship with young men of noble line like Louis d'Albuféra, Gabriel de La Rochefoucauld, Bertrand de Fénelon, Antoine Bibesco, Georges de Lauris, Armand de Guiche. Some of these, like Comte Bertrand de Salignac-Fénelon and the Rumanian Prince Antoine Bibesco, were in the diplomatic service: all were well connected and rich, but beyond this they shared with Proust a passion for literature and the arts, went with him on journeys to visit the churches, cathedrals and other architectures within motoring distance of Paris, and show that in selecting such friends of intelligent worth and taste, his attendance on Society had not been intellectually barren. Furthermore, this section of golden Parisian youth merged into the character of Saint-Loup in the novel, with the accent perhaps on Fénelon. Louis d'Albuféra was the lover of an actress Louisa de Mornand with whom Proust struck up a friendship of a peculiarly intimate nature, whose remaining evidences lead one to believe that he might have had some sort of carnal relationship with her. Probably she formed part of the pattern for the character Rachel, mistress of Saint-Loup, and otherwise she may have been reflected in Albertine.

(*Left*) A medallion of Prince Emmanuel Bibesco. (*Right*) Prince Antoine Bibesco. These two Rumanian noblemen, rich and aesthetically gifted, were friends of Proust at the turn of the century and later.

In 1900, when that frilled and verdigris-green-painted Art Nouveau entrance to the new Métro at the Etoile was erected to mark the Great Exposition, the Proust family moved to a larger apartment in the rue de Courcelles, grander new *salons* of approaching death. Proust *père* died in 1903 ; *The Bible of Amiens* was published in 1904, and not much noted in the Press. Then in 1905 there came the fatal passing of the possessive and long-suffering widow and mother. After this, Proust's first move was to a nursing-home for neuropaths, the first time he had taken such a step.

The death of a father such as the honoured and large figure of the professor-doctor removes from an oedipal situation a naturally important ingredient: and even if one does not subscribe to such sexually based jealousy, the father-figure of final authority, the being with the final 'No', is gone. Leaving, in either case, an ambivalent sense of relief and vacuum. The loss of his mother was to Proust plainly a deeper wound, of fundamental effect on his disposition, his work and his life. The two of them had always been most closely attached. Mme Proust took infinite pains to comfort her son in his illness. Over the years she ran errands, watched at his door, ordered the house and the servants in such a way as to ensure quiet and rest for the invalid. Proust, involved with her in a classic condition of love-hate, took advantage of this. Whenever she did not measure up to her own remarkable standards of self-sacrifice, he would be likely to complain. Quarrels ensued, the kinds of quarrel which are made up less of a wish to put something right than simply to exercise the need of having each an effect on the other, marking the other with a loving scar, continuing interminably in this reiterant self-indulgence which finds a strange pleasure in provoking pain. Not that otherwise there was not a deep and affirmative love between them – the two extremes go hand in hand. Whether or not, as has been suggested, Proust wore his mother to death is open to question; many a troubled and tenacious mother has died in her due course of independent illness. But Proust thought he had killed her. This is echoed in his essay on the filial sentiments of a parricide (*Pastiches et mélanges*), which pretty plainly confirmed his feelings of guilt. He wrote it first for *Le Figaro* after an acquaintance, Henri van Blarenberghe, had murdered his mother and then com-mitted suicide. Both murder and suicide were particularly appalling in their violent details: and it was Proust's purpose to show that such a murder could be paralleled by what all men do to their mothers in a less violent but equally certain way, day after day, year after year, by the anxiety they cause throughout a loving mother's life. If they could see the slow disintegration they cause, if they could realize it in a split second like van Blarenberghe when he saw his mother bleed to death, they too would shoot themselves.

Nevertheless, and in spite of his grief, the way now lay clear for a

(*Opposite*) Louisa de Mornand in 1901. She was an actress and the mistress of Proust's friend, the Marquis Louis d'Albuféra; and probably also an intimate love and inspiration of Proust himself.

more open approach in his writing to the analysis of affairs of family and homosexuality; there was no one now to hurt. (Except brother Robert, who is conveniently left out of the novel.) He left Dr Sollier's nursing-home quickly, after only six weeks; he was both too intelligent for the Doctor, and too fond of his illness. A neurotic writer hates to have his own personality, which he may rightly believe to be the fount of his art, tampered with, however miserable his condition. An insight as to how miserable that condition was even before his mother died is given in a letter to Mme Straus in the spring of 1905:

I am worn out by letters from Montesquiou. Every time he gives a reading or a fête etc., etc., he *refuses* to admit that I am sick, and beforehand there are summonses, threats, visits from d'Yturri, who wakes me up, and, afterwards, there are reproaches for not having gone. I believe it would still be possible to get well if it weren't for '*les autres*'. But the exhaustion they cause you, one's helplessness at making them understand the suffering – sometimes lasting a month – that follows the fool-hardiness one has committed for the sake of what they imagine to be a great pleasure: all that is death.

In 1906 he gave up his parents' rue de Courcelles apartment and stayed for several months, August to December, in Versailles, before finally taking over at 102 Boulevard Haussmann, a house partly belonging to an aunt. At the Hôtel des Réservoirs in Versailles he occupied a large and lofty room hung with tapestries, a room fit more for the historical guide than to live and sleep in. But sleep in it he did and in fact seldom left the room for those five months, missing

Grand Hôtel, Cabourg. The motor-car shown is old and reliable; but newer and speedier kinds were coming in.

altogether both the beauties of the Palace and its Trianons and the autumnal drama of the trees in the park. It was again a voluntary incarceration, though consoled by the visits of friends and invigorated by arranging, at a distance and with the help of his brother and friends, the forthcoming move to the Boulevard Haussmann. Not much is known of his work at Versailles: but probably the sounds and scents of this garrison town lent their atmosphere to his later descriptions of Doncières in the novel.

By the year 1907 his mourning was relieved, as often happens, by new accesses of freedom – in this case, several published articles of worth, and, on a frivolous plane, investigatory visits to heterosexual brothels (it must be remembered, a Frenchman went to a brothel much as an Englishman went to his club – to escape the routine of home-life, to drink and talk in a convivial atmosphere). Also that year, with his new part-time secretary, Robert Ulrich, there began the succession of young homosexual servants who throughout his life thenceforth were to be kept in his places of residence, half-seen by visitors as silent prisoners in the shadows. He revisited Cabourg in August: there he confirmed his impressions for the novel's seaside scenes, and there he met the chauffeur Alfred Agostinelli.

For some weeks he went motoring with this handsome young mechanic who looked in his cape and helmet like 'a nun of speed', playing like St Cecilia on the organ pedals of the gears. Proust felt himself to be leading 'the life of a cannon-ball in flight'. He had taken quickly to the motor-car, because as an ill man he welcomed the ease

Alfred Agostinelli, the chauffeur whom Proust employed in and around Cabourg in 1907.

(*Left*) The Dieppe Circuit (1908). Enthusiastic young mechanics like Agostinelli were driving France fast ahead of other motoring-minded countries.

Eragny, landscape by Camille Pissarro (1895). When Proust was motored past the steeples of Caen, he sensed something similar to this – a steepled mystery which, in his novel, became the episode of Martinville.

it provided (incidentally dispensing with the asthmatic exudations of the horse) and, of course, because it introduced a new race of personable young 'mechanics'. On one of these journeys in 1907 he saw the moving steeples of Caen, later to take their part in the evocative steeples of the narrator's Martinville. In the novel, on a boyhood drive to Combray, the narrator is pleasantly startled to observe how three distant steeples change places and appearance as the road winds and affects their distant aspect. In a strange way familiar to most travellers, they seem to become animate, and, imbued with this odd dancing life, hold some sort of attractive mystery never to be explained. But the sight is enough to suggest that material things need not be dull but all contain a life of their own, changing according to the eye of the beholder. Here space rather than time is the element, although time is also involved in the carriage's speed. In any case, the excitant factor

is change. And this may even have suggested to Proust his technique throughout the novel of making his characters change their attitudes and essences, not only because of the passage of time but also because of a concealed disposition to change innate within them. Nothing, nobody is fixed or understandable.

Later, in 1912, in a letter to Antoine Bibesco, he writes of the same kind of experience, linking characters with the passing of time, space:

Then, like a city which, while the train pursues its winding course, seems to be first on our right, then on our left, the varying aspects the same character will have assumed to such a degree that they will have made him seem like successive and different characters, will project – but only in that one way – the sensation of time passed. Such characters will later reveal themselves as different from what they were in the present, different from what one believes them to be, a circumstance which, indeed, occurs frequently enough in life.

Mlle Yvonne Lerolle, by Maurice Denis (1897). A study in three aspects, suggesting that nobody is fixed or understandable. This was a favourite theme of Proust.

(*Left*) Notre-Dame de Saint-Lô, by
John Ruskin (1848).

(*Right*) *West façade of Rouen Cathedral*,
by Claude Monet (1894). Proust
made many visits to such
architectural points of interest.

With this vision of the Martinville steeples, the young narrator also has
his first experience of the power of art over these mysteries: he writes an
essay on them, and in doing so finds immediate release.

Between now and the middle of 1909 other expeditions were made
– the last circuitous advances to the real beginnings of the writing of
A la recherche. These were unsatisfactory approaches to the novel
itself; and he began the extraordinary half-critical, half-autobio-
graphical essays which were to be published years later as *Contre
Sainte-Beuve* (on the premise that you cannot assess a writer by his
outward personality and life, but must search for deeper sensibilities,
intuition being so much more important than the intellect); and a
brilliant series of parodies of the work of writers like Flaubert and
Renan, a maniacally joyful outburst from a manic-depressive, high
comedy indeed and the first written precursor to all the humour with
which the bittersweetness of *A la recherche* is so refreshingly laced. At
the same time the homosexual Eulenburg Affair broke in Berlin: the
pacifist and francophile Prince Philip von Eulenburg, close friend
of General Cuno von Moltke and the Kaiser, was accused of homosexuality, and politically ruined. The publicity given to these goings-
on at 'Sodom-on-Spree' was a further stimulation to Proust's interest
in the 'accursed race' and ultimately reinforced the Sodomitic chapters
of *A la recherche*.

On some day in the New Year of 1909, he had been given a cup of tea and a bit of toast. The toast was dipped – and a moment of stupendous vision experienced: the recall to childhood, when he had tasted something similar with his grandfather at Auteuil, was mysteriously, ecstatically complete – or should one rather say, the mystery was ended, the mnemonic mystery at last solved by *realization*. This 'realization' is a matter which affects all our lives some of the time. Very broadly, we spend our time in habitual acceptance, accepting what we have been told about things, accepting our experience of things, accepting agreed theories and ideas – and then on one unexpected day, in some fortuitous state of calm or heightened nervous perception, in one held moment like the momentous still centre of a great storm, we suddenly see some action or series of objects as very clearly themselves, outside all preconception, with a clinical virgin vision. This moment of vision can be brought about by involuntary memory, memory induced not by any mental process but by the more intimate senses themselves. The senses re-experience a thing completely, outside habit, free of all mentally trained reflexes. It can be anything, a sad love-affair, a landscape, penury, the corner of a room, a boot. With most people the moment is intense, but allowed to pass as having little practical use. With great painters and poets, the moment is recognized as invaluable – and, as far as can be done, the mind is trained *against* habit to allow for the miraculous intervention of such accesses of perception. Thus, attempts at painting a boot can be very ordinary – and then suddenly sublime, as we may see in paintings of single simple objects such as Dürer's *Praying Hands*, Hokusai's *Wave*, Van Gogh's ordinary but infinite chair at Arles. This is the result not only of technique, not only of conscious will – there is something else much stronger at work. It is a vision difficult to convey in words. One of the most concise but necessarily still vague definitions I know is that of a Taoist teacher who went on a journey for several years, and was asked on his return what he had seen. He replied: 'Everywhere I went, I saw *that*ness.'

So, in his thirty-ninth year, Proust had his apocalyptic minute of thatness, magically illuminating the mystery of memory which had nagged at him throughout his writing life, and which was to illuminate thereafter the next creative, laborious, painful and ecstatic thirteen years until his death. The simple tea-and-toast brought back in an instant, like that re-reeling of a whole lifetime said to be the last lot of a drowning man, his whole childhood in immense and trans-cendental detail. It was the great confirmation, for Proust, of the truth of 'involuntary' memory.

Ever since his student days, possibly before, the curious pleasure of memory had perplexed him. He had a suspicion that time does not really pass; and there were to be echoing problems of the value of what is thought to be illusion above reality, and of the whole nature of art, a product of life superior to living. Now in a late-flowering receptive moment he perceived, on a random winter's day, the answer. That word 'perceived' should be underlined a dozen times. For he had experienced the sensation before, as many of us have always done; as writers as various as Chateaubriand, Nerval, Wilkie Collins, the Danish J. A. Larsen, have recorded in passing detail. Only – with Proust it did not pass. It was recognized once and for all as the key, as far as he was concerned, to everything. It was his moment of absolute vision. He netted it. And the final writing of *A la recherche* was conceived. For other writers, other themes: for Proust, this was the end-all of a lifetime's quest.

Many ingredients of the story were already there: some of them had been written in various draft forms, four or even more times already. Instances like the refusal of his mother's good-night kiss, or like earlier seaside memories, were obviously obsessive with him – insoluble but mysteriously powerful, he had nagged and dragged away at them with a bulldog tenacity, if such can be said of one described as looking like 'yesterday's gardenia'. However, such mysteries had hitherto proved sterile, suggesting no theme of hope, but witness only to the pessimist view that all we love turns to nothing with the satiety of desire. Now, it would be different. No single matter is turned to nothing. Everything is preserved in the memory: not to be recalled at will, but by involuntary chance. Within each of our sensibilities, properly cultivated, lies the possibility of a return to golden moments of the past, which have never in fact passed because they have remained alive in us all the time, and are now the better, purer, clearer for the suppression of the dross of habit and daily living which clouded their reality at the time. As Proust wrote, essentially: 'The true paradises are the paradises we have lost' – meaning, of course, which we have never lost, but have only temporarily neglected.

Thus he found the means to make his story – mostly parallel to his own life story – affirmative. Humanity always hopes for an affirmative explanation of what seems the inescapable pointlessness of life. It is the same instinct, immensely magnified, of the sentimental theatre-goer for a happy ending. Consequently *A la recherche*, in spite of some first appearances, in spite of hundreds of pages devoted to looking at human deficiency in the starkest of eyeballs – *A la recherche* is a contented book.

Sixty sleepless hours when the electric light was never switched off are recorded of Proust at the beginning of July 1909: it seems that this may have been the moment of the great plunge. Certainly it was thereabouts that the contemporary essays of *Contre Sainte-Beuve* came to a stop. It had been earlier in this year that he made inquiries as to whether the name 'Guermantes' could be used in a novel. In June he

wrote to Montesquiou that he had undertaken a long work, 'a sort of novel'. And in August, from Cabourg, he wrote to Mme Straus: 'I have just begun – and finished – a whole long book.' That was the first recorded instance of any part of the mysterious work reaching completion. His departure for Cabourg had been delayed (by exhaustion brought on by overwork?) until the third week of August; and once by the sea he eschewed it, working through the night until long after dawn, not rising to appear in public until dark and dinner-time. The public with whom he then consorted for his short leisure hours provides a small mystery: certainly it involved a number of young men at the Casino, but as certainly it included young women, grown-up girls in fact, to whom he gave expensive presents and affectionate and playful extensions of his company. Months previously he had told a friend of his feeling for 'young girls – as if life were not complicated enough already'. Also, there had been vague but trenchant hints of marriage to someone never named. Perhaps these newish interests confirm his at least spiritual bisexuality; or a wish for normality and acceptance; or perhaps, once again, it is the bulldog in the gardenia – the author at work taking pains to sniff out his raw material, in this case the Albertine-to-be and her little band of girls.

A pastel called *Memories*, by Fernand Khnopff (1889). It gives an impression of the sportive young women of Cabourg who attracted Proust, and also of his sometimes statuesque characters – momentarily arrested, yearning for the past to be present.

(*Below*) Félix Mayol, witty and effeminate singer, to whose café-concert Proust used to go, in light but fascinated mood, *c.* 1911.

Returned to Paris alone, he took formal leave of many of his friends and re-entered the cloister of work. The speed of writing – or in his case, often rewriting – is undetermined; but that year the Combray chapter at least was finished. His isolation continued into the next year, and throughout a particular and extra insulation by the Seine, whose extraordinary January floods reached right up as far as his Haussmann doorstep. Small matters mark the absorbed author – like many another, he relegated food to no more than a regular régime, eating the same things day after day. As was his custom for many years, he drank great quantities of strong black coffee. It was the year 1910 when the Ballets Russes took firm root in Paris, and this indeed lured him out, enchanted him. Then to Cabourg again, and a further bout of work, while in Paris he had ordered the installation of sound-proof cork-lining for his walls: it was not unique, others had it, but it was more effective than other sound preventions known to the time, like baized study doors, like kitchen doors baized against the clatter of crockery.

In 1911 he had eight hundred pages ready for publication. There are various glimpses of him at about this time – at a new play of d'Annunzio's, or in lighter mood at Félix Mayol's concert hall, or owl-eyed and terrifying at a great Paris ball, or at the Golf Club Ball at Cabourg, or loitering palely on the links in a violet velvet cloak. But mostly he

The Seine flood of 1910. This shows
the Quai des Grands-Augustins,
near to the river; but the water went
as far on the other bank as Proust's
Boulevard Haussmann, complicating
further his insulated life.

A design by Léon Bakst (1910).
Bakst produced many designs for the
Ballets Russes, influencing women's
fashions, Paris and Proust.

Vaslav Nijinsky and Ida Rubinstein
in the ballet *Schéhérazade*, painted by
Georges Barbier (1911).

Manuscript of the last page of *A la recherche*, to which Proust, after writing the word 'Temps', has added 'Fin'.

was at work. And it is generally considered that in these years both the volumes to be known as *Du côté de chez Swann* (*Swann's Way*) and some of the final essences of *Le Temps retrouvé* (*Time Regained*) were completed, together with a smaller version of *A l'ombre des jeunes filles en fleurs* (*Within a Budding Grove*). Thus the beginning and the end first, leaving the vast work to expand within itself as mnemonic Time – and the years of real time – were to dictate.

There was now to follow a long and complicated search for publishers. Proust was up against it from the first because of the lack of plot and action in his work, for publishers were still concerned with the narrative and plot legacy of novels of the previous century: not yet the years of streams of consciousness. Publication in France depended upon a mixture of commercial acumen, diplomatic advances and friendly recommendation: all this took its allotted time,

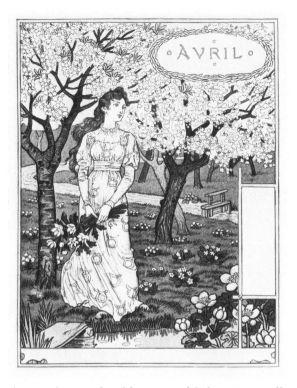

April, by Eugène Grasset (1896). This calendar illustration reflects Proust's feeling for the flowering of young girls, coupled with his childhood memories of Eastertide and walks by the mysterious river at Illiers.

and in due course the novel was refused by two publishers, Fasquelle and the Nouvelle Revue Française in the person of André Gide. Memories of Proust's old reputation as a *salon* socialite played against him; he was regarded as an amateur, and in fact the typescript was scarcely read by the N.R.F., a fact for which Gide much later rebuked himself profoundly. Then a third publisher, Ollendorff, rejected the book, saying that he was unable to comprehend why the author needed thirty pages to describe how he turned over in bed before going to sleep. The intrigue had to begin all over again. Finally, since Proust now offered to pay the expenses of publication, Grasset agreed. (Later, Grasset confessed that he did not even read the manuscript!) Publication of *Du côté de chez Swann* became due for November 1913.

But in the meantime he had fallen in love. Deeply emotional love-affairs had for some years been sublimated by the death of his mother and the birth of his novel: now, coincident with the recession of these all-absorbing emotional events, his old Cabourg chauffeur of 1908, Alfred Agostinelli, appeared on the doorstep asking for a job. Proust already had a chauffeur: but was moved suddenly to make Agostinelli his secretary. Agostinelli told him he was now married, with the result that both he and his wife (whom Proust never liked) were invited to move in at 102 Boulevard Haussmann, an immediate blueprint for unhappiness. Agostinelli was a Monégasque of Italian descent. His face in photographs ominously mirrors the round and dark eyes of his captivated master, who now proceeded to make him a 'captive' in his household, and thus laid the foundations, it is generally thought, for the conception of the imprisoned Albertine.

Meanwhile, proofs were arriving from Grasset: and Proust began immediately to rewrite the book on the proofs, adding and gumming on strips of paper in a manner which became his habit and finally produced those extraordinary manuscript pages sometimes two metres in length.

Besides expanding narrative and descriptions, he was always worried about the accuracy of details. He went to immense pains to be sure of facts outside the sphere of his own personal knowledge, for instance on dressmaking or botany. We find him writing to Lucien Daudet, who had already read *Swann's Way* at an earlier stage, in the following terms:

About the flowers, I assure you, I have many doubts; for instance, in the first version of the hawthorns (which appeared in *Le Figaro*) there were wild roses on the same road. But having discovered in Bonnier's *Botany* that roses do not bloom until later, I made a correction and put in the book 'not until a few weeks later could one see, etc.' As for the verbena and heliotrope, it is true that Bonnier points out that the former blooms from June to October, the latter from June to August! But since Bonnier is dealing with wild flowers, I thought (and the horticulturist to whom I wrote assured me) that in a garden (and not wild like thornbush or wild rose) they could be made to bloom in May while the hawthorns are still in bloom.

In this considerable rewriting at proof stage it is notable how money can play its part in the making of a particular work of art. A writer less well endowed could not possibly have afforded such extensive correction; nor, of course, the initial ability to pay publication expenses. Then again, commercial aspects intervened in the actual compilation of the volume. How long should it be, to make it a viable proposition to the reading public? Proust experimented by removing whole chunks from one part to another in the book, in search of a suitable ending to a volume of the right length for the bookshops. So much for the inviolably sensitive concentric plan of the writer . . . though it must be remembered also that, faced with such limitations, it is the writer who still remains in aesthetic charge of the work, and re-reading and re-thinking can also beget improvement. And beyond such detailed changes there certainly was and always had been a con-centric plan. In February 1913 he states this in a letter to René Blum:

I don't know whether I have told you that this book is a novel. At least it deviates least from the novel form. There is a Monsieur who narrates and who says 'I'; there are a great many characters; in the first volume they are 'prepared' in such a way that what they do in the second is exactly the opposite of what one would expect from the first. . . . And from the point of view of composition, it is so complex that it will not be clear until much later when all the 'themes' have begun to be combined.

(*Opposite*) A proof showing how heavy were Proust's continual corrections. It may be traced to page 22 of *Swann's Way*

Aussi, comme ma grand'tante en usait cavalièrement avec lui. Comme elle croyait qu'il devait être flatté par nos invitations et trouvait naturel qu'il arrivât souvent avec un panier de framboises ou de pêches de son jardin, et qu'il nous eût rapporté de Padoue des photographies des Vertus et des Vices du Giotto, qui lui reste ne m'avait pas plu, l'Envie ayant l'air de sucer son serpent, et la Charité se déhanchant pour que Dieu puisse attraper son cœur; de l'Abraham de B. Gozzoli.

On ne se gênait guère pour lui faire pousser le piano et tourner les pages les soirs où la sœur de ma grand'mère chantait, pour l'envoyer quérir qu'on avait besoin d'une recette de civet de chasseur, de perdreau à la crapaudine, de salade d'ananas, de sandwich, ou rester pour les dîners d'œufs de ténèbres au où on ne l'invitait pas, ne lui trouvant pas un prestige suffisant pour qu'on pût le servir à des étrangers qui venaient pour la première fois. Si la conversation tombait sur les Princes de la Maison de France: « des gens que nous ne connaîtrons jamais ni vous ni moi et nous en passons, n'est-ce pas, disait ma grand'tante à Swann qui avait peut-être dans sa poche une lettre de Polsdorf; et elle maniait avec une brusquerie et avec des façons comiques cet être précieux, comme s'il se plaisait Pamasar et de qui se prêtait aux longs soirs comme un bibelot de collection qu'il brûlerait comme un jouet bon marché. C'est que même au point de vue des plus insignifiantes choses de la vie, nous ne sommes pas un tout matériellement constitué, identique pour tout le monde, et dont chacun n'a qu'à aller prendre connaissance, comme d'un acte de l'état civil ou d'un testament; notre personnalité sociale est une création de la pensée des autres et le Swann que connurent à la même époque tant ma grand'tante, quand le soir, dans le petit jardin de Combray, après qu'avaient retenti les deux coups hésitants

de la clochette, elle injectait et vivifiait de tout ce qu'elle savait sur la famille Swann, l'obscur et incertain personnage qui se détachait suivi de ma grand'mère, sur un fond de ténèbres et qu'on ne reconnaissait qu'à la voix. « voir une personne que nous connaissons » est en partie un acte intellectuel. Nous remplissons l'apparence physique de l'être que nous voyons de toutes les notions que nous avons sur lui et dans l'aspect total que nous nous représentons, ces notions ont certainement la plus grande part. Elles finissent par gonfler les joues, par suivre en une adhérence si exacte la ligne du nez, elles se mêlent si bien de nuancer la sonorité de la voix comme si celle-ci n'était qu'une transparente enveloppe, que chaque fois que nous voyons ce visage et que nous entendons cette voix, ce sont ces notions que nous retrouvons, regardons, que nous écoutons. Sans doute, dans le Swann qu'ils s'étaient constitué, mes parents avaient négligé de faire entrer une foule de particularités de sa vie mondaine qui étaient cause que d'autres personnes, quand elles étaient en sa présence, voyaient les élégances régner dans son visage et s'arrêter à son nez busqué comme à leur frontière habituelle; Mais comme par ignorance, ils n'avaient pu loger en Swann le honni autour de ses amis illustres, l'écho des fêtes fastueuses dont il était le centre et l'attrait, ils avaient entassé dans son visage vacant au fond de ses yeux dépréciés le vague et doux séjour mi-mémoire, mi-oubli des heures oisives passées ensemble après nos dîners hebdomadaires, autour de la table de jeu ou au jardin, toute notre vie de bon voisinage campagnard. L'enveloppe vivante de notre ami en avait été si bien bourrée, ainsi que de quelques souvenirs relatifs à ses parents, que ce Swann-là, était devenu un être vrai, pas plus que l'autre, on n'aurait pu détruire. Plus bonhomme, sans doute, plus simple, était il moins réel que l'élé-

Les premiers doutes de mes grands-parents à l'égard de la situation de Villeparisis, de l'illustre maison de Bouillon, qui avait été élevée au Sacré-Cœur avec ma grand'... Elles s'étaient un peu perdues de vue, Mme de Villeparisis aimait ma grand'mère et si celle-ci, à cause de sa conception des castes... résiste à ses prières d'échanger des visites avec elle elle savait en revanche que si elle avait un service à demander elle était toujours sûre de trouver dans sa vieille amie le plus solide appui; ma grand'mère nous la dépeignait comme une femme d'une intelligence supérieure, peu sensible, peu aimable, avare de son affection, attachant du prix à ses moindres entretiens à ses billets qui étaient courts mais exquis; mais aussi quand elle avait promis de faire une démarche... ma grand'mère, qui la savait proche parente du maréchal de Mac-Mahon, avait cet plusieurs fois la prier d'intervenir auprès de lui en faveur d'amis à nous — mettant à tenir sa promesse une promptitude, une intelligence, une discrétion, une efficacité admirables.

Chaque fois que ma grand'mère eut ainsi à aller la voir, Mme de Villeparisis l'avait poussée à louer un appartement dans la même maison qu'elle ou dans une des maisons contiguës et semblables sur toutes donnaient sur des jardins d'autant plus naturels à eux, qu'aucun jardinier ne s'en occupait et dont ma grand'mère était revenue chaque fois plus enthousiaste ainsi que d'une fleuriste qui avait sa boutique et dont les filles faisaient aussi des réparations de broderies

grand'mère était entrée demander qu'on fit un point à sa jupe qu'elle avait déchirée dans l'escalier. Ma grand'mère avait trouvé ces gens, le fleuriste et sa fille parfaits, elle déplaçait que la petite était une perle et que le fleuriste était l'homme le plus distingué, le mieux, qu'elle eut jamais vu. Car pour ma grand'mère, la distinction était quelque chose d'absolument indépendant du rang social. Elle s'extasiait sur les lettres d'une ouvrière en disant à maman: « Sévigné n'aurait pas mieux dit ! » et en revanche, d'un neveu de Mme de Villeparisis qu'elle avait rencontré chez elle : « Ah ! ma fille, comme il est commun ! »

Mme de Villeparisis, au cours d'une de ses trois ou quatre visites, qui furent toutes que ma grand'mère lui fit pendant les quarante années qui s'écoulèrent depuis la sortie du Sacré-Cœur, lui dit une fois, « Je crois que vous connaissez beaucoup M. Swann qui est un grand ami de mes neveux Villebon. » Ma grand'mère n'avait pas osé demander de détails, mais cette nouvelle qu'elle nous rapporta en rougissant, eut pour effet non pas d'élever M. Swann, mais d'abaisser les neveux Villebon sur l'échelle de notre estima mondaine et surtout d'exciter chez ma grand'tante contre Mme de Villeparisis une mauvaise humeur dont ma grand'mère était éclaboussée. Il semblait que la considération que nous accordions à Mme de Villeparisis lui créât le devoir de ne rien faire qui l'en rendit moins digne, et qu'elle avait manqué à ce devoir en apprenant l'existence de Swann et en permettant à des parents à elle de le fréquenter. Quant à ma grand'mère n'en eut où elle venait de reconnaître qu'elle nous avait trompés sur la valeur de la personne que nous avions placée si haut au foi de ses récits; et l'idée erronée que mes grands-parents se faisaient des relations de Swann n'ayant pas été rectifiée par

A portrait of André Gide, by Jacques-Emile Blanche (1912). Gide was eventually to become Proust's publisher, though he originally turned down *Swann's Way*.

Excerpts of *Swann's Way* had been published in *Le Figaro*, and now when it was finally published on 14 November 1913, several excellent reviews were engineered, ensuring the book's second edition in December. But – 'engineered'? Although some were written by his friends, they would certainly have been written honestly and with deep feeling for the work: a certain explicit etiquette in Parisian literary circles, a jockeying for position and a to and fro of letters of recommendation, must be accepted as normal. This can be illustrated by a letter from Proust to a literary friend as far back as 1905. He writes:

... When I did *La Bible d'Amiens*, I thought my literary friends would take the utmost pains for me. The preface was dedicated to Léon Daudet, who writes for *Le Gaulois*, for *L'Echo*, etc.; I let it be hinted to him that an article would be acceptable to me. *Never a word, not an allusion*, no mention of my name in articles where he mentions everybody in the world. Don't say anything, but I still haven't swallowed it.

Now Gide read the book properly, and wrote apologizing for the biggest error in his life in refusing it: and his company, the N.R.F., expressed their readiness to publish the two succeeding volumes. An impasse, thus, with Grasset; but this was a problem whose solution had fortuitously to be postponed by the beginning of war.

Proust's pleasure in the book's reception was impaired by the unhappiness of his affair – if affair it ever was – with Agostinelli. His jealousy became an habitual anguish. Jealousy he had already in past years known and written about; this with Agostinelli was more a

88

confirmation than an inspiration of all the involved sentiments which shadow and illuminate the narrator's torture with the novel's imprisoned Albertine.

Proust was no doubt unbearably possessive; but in any case Agostinelli was a young mechanic-engineer of the times, and his interest turned to the new national expertise in aviation, in which France led the world. Although Proust refused to help him learn to fly, he allowed himself to be driven to small aerodromes near Paris, where the two of them met young aviators and from which, eventually, were born those beautiful descriptions of a contemporary phenomenon – the first aeroplanes in the sky. Aeroplanes – from the man who so faithfully recorded the great drawing-rooms of the *belle époque* . . . here is an essence again of the strangely contrasting period interests in Proust's life and work. And the aeroplane itself was to mean the end of Agostinelli's service with Proust, and finally the end of himself in a crash.

(*Left*) Poster for a big aviation week in Champagne (1909). It was an era when France led the world in aviation.

(*Right*) Poster for an aviation concourse in Monte-Carlo (1909). Alfred Agostinelli, Proust's chauffeur and secretary and friend, flew to his death in the sea near Antibes, a few miles along the coast from Monte-Carlo.

89

Armée de Paris,
Habitants de Paris,

Les Membres du Gouvernement de la
République ont quitté Paris pour donner
une impulsion nouvelle à la défense
nationale.

J'ai reçu le mandat de défendre Paris
contre l'envahisseur.

Ce mandat, je le remplirai jusqu'au bout.

Paris, le 3 Septembre 1914

Le Gouverneur Militaire de Paris,
Commandant l'Armée de Paris,

GALLIÉNI

Paris – Imprimerie MARCEL PICARD, 100, rue du Faubourg-Saint-Martin (Tél. 112-74 et 432-73)

The military government of Paris
issued this *mandat* on 3 September
1914. By then, the capital was severely
threatened by German invasion.

Not long after the publication of *Swann's Way*, Agostinelli left
Proust to learn flying near his native Monaco in the south, and thereby
spoiled the days which should have been gladdened by the success of
his book. In May 1914, Proust's torment of jealousy was to turn to
black grief at the news that the young aviator's plane had crashed in
the sea. It occurred only a few hundred yards out at Antibes, but the
aviator – curiously enrolled under the pseudonym of Marcel Swann –
could not swim and was drowned. The whole Agostinelli episode –
love, captivity, jealousy, escape, death – must have been deeply and
painfully felt by the writer: but since he was that writer, it was also
recorded, and finally transposed into the very similar story of Albertine
in the novel.

In June–July excerpts from *Le Côté de Guermantes* (*The Guermantes
Way*) were published in the *Nouvelle Revue Française*; but it was the
doomed year of war, the first year of the scything down of Europe's
men of fighting age; and thoughts of things like further publication –
for instance a further volume, *Within a Budding Grove*, scheduled for
October – had to be put aside in the vast and general upheaval.
Mobilization affected most sectors of life, certainly that of his printers;

Reynaldo Hahn (standing) at the wintry Western Front in the First World War.

(*Below*) Proust's doctor-brother, Robert, in uniform and on leave.

in a minor way Proust's friends of the *gratin* suffered a major casualty in the sudden disappearance of servants; his other friends of the aesthetic élite began to be dispersed into various services. As a sick man himself he could do nothing, and his immediate personal life was discomfited by changes in the household services he relied upon. Against the greater catastrophe, these sound trivial, but to a man so ill they must have seemed momentous. He was, in fact, lucky enough to have Céleste Albaret, the wife of his old chauffeur Odilon, come to live in with him. Odilon now provided him with the services of a taxi, while Céleste acted as both housekeeper and secretary.

In August the German armies broke through Belgium, and then the French and British lines, and arrived thirty miles from a Paris already evacuated by upwards of a million people. Proust remained day after day, worried about his brother and his friends, and by his own powerlessness. Finally he took train with Céleste in the habitual direction of Cabourg. He stayed that September at his old Grand Hôtel by the Monet sea, among a scattering of old friends like Mme Straus, and the newly wounded in the local hospital. In October he returned to Paris where he remained for the rest of the war, working and revising the enormous interstices of his long novel. He wanted to serve in some way, but was too ill to do so. Yet he was an avid observer of the war from a tower certainly not of ivory; and his natural effort was to proceed with the only work on hand, which over the momentous cloistered years grew longer and longer, and changed substantially as now his characters were allowed to grow older and the war itself entered and altered the pages. An immensely improved work, in fact the masterpiece we know, was the end result, an unsought and fortuitous turn of the fortunes of war in that extraordinary cork-lined factory in the Boulevard Haussmann.

One outstanding clue remains to show his progress on the novel. At the end of 1915 Mme Scheikévitch, a hostess of literary interests, gave him her copy of *Swann's Way* to be autographed. She must have discussed the novel with Proust in some detail, for he now returned the book with the blank pages covered in his writing. This turned out to be a complete résumé of the entire story of Albertine, just as it was finally published. Not only was he thus far ahead with either his planning or writing, but he was now concerning himself not so much with distant memories as with the immediate past and his present reaction to it – in fact the loss of Alfred Agostinelli and his feelings first of jealousy surviving death and secondly the slow oblivion with which such a pain was healed, loss of a loss.

Against the great and violent picture of these years, it seems odd to read of the ordinary matters of life continuing at home in the capital away from the Front. But continue, at various levels, they do. In the course of the years a change of publishers from Grasset to Gide's N.R.F. was negotiated. And there are many strange, almost unbelievable episodes related of Proust, like his suddenly increased concentration on music, and the way at midnight he dug out the Quatuor Poulet to play for him César Franck's music alone in his apartment: Zeppelins and Gothas above, yet driving in a cab round

(*Left*) Père Noël near the roof of the Ritz Hotel in Paris.

(*Right*) A Christmas Eve menu at the Ritz. In spite of bombardment, much of Parisian life continued as usual.

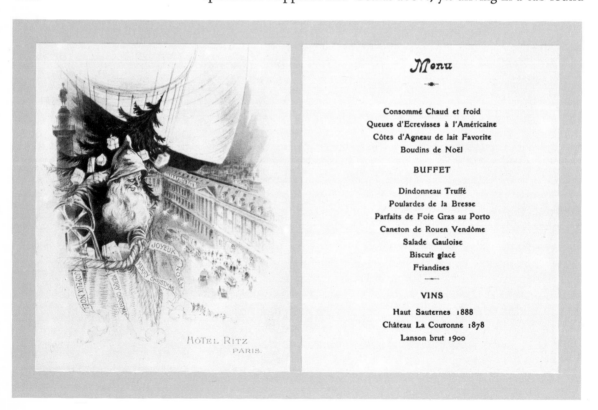

Menu

Consommé Chaud et froid
Queues d'Ecrevisses à l'Américaine
Côtes d'Agneau de lait Favorite
Boudins de Noël

BUFFET

Dindonneau Truffé
Poulardes de la Bresse
Parfaits de Foie Gras au Porto
Caneton de Rouen Vendôme
Salade Gauloise
Biscuit glacé
Friandises

VINS

Haut Sauternes 1888
Château La Couronne 1878
Lanson brut 1900

HÔTEL RITZ
PARIS.

the blacked-out streets picking up 'cellists and violinists from their beds – a weird effort on the part of a white-faced invalid, almost hilarious had it not so serious a reason, field observation of musical perceptions for the novel's beautifully evocative Vinteuil septet. Compared with our present age of press-button music, this illustrates the importance then of performed music – the barrel-organ, the ballad sung at the piano, the passing military band were not minor or laughable noises but valued occasions. The pianola was not enough.

Again and again the invalid Proust had shown these sudden moments of effort. His persistence was extraordinary – suddenly driving to observe apple trees in blossom outside Paris, or the passing autumnal moments of the trees in the Bois de Boulogne, fits of a novelist's momentary anxiety that he cannot quite live the memory of such phenomena, and so construct its sensuous essence. At the same time he risked further illness by such exposure to different atmospheres. But this kind of sick man was never confined wholly to bed. He was often up at sundown, or later: and in 1917 began his reputation as Proust of the Ritz, treating that hotel as a second home and escape from the indefatigable work- and sick-room. The richly appointed Ritz offered a phantom echo of the grand *salons* of the past, and an atmosphere of discreet and affable servants; and there he found old and

The Ritz Hotel, in the Place Vendôme in Paris. In 1917 Proust, iller and more tired than ever, used it both as an escape and as a second home for his memories.

new friends, including among the latter the Rumanian-Greek Princess Soutzo, the affianced of Paul Morand, once again a spirited and elegant woman betrothed to a friend, and thus as usual with Proust approachable but unattainable. Progressively more extraordinary in appearance, iller and his clothes scruffier, he was nevertheless extraordinarily good company, entertaining his friends with long and gifted literary disquisitions far into the night: he was also good company for the staff, whom he tipped extravagantly as always. Once, for instance, being without ready money at the end of an evening, he asked the doorman at the Ritz whether he might borrow fifty francs from him. And when the doorman complied, pressed the money back into his hands, saying, 'Keep them. They were for you.' Of course, the debt was repaid the next day.

The Princess Soutzo, of Rumania and Greece, whose elegance and intelligence attracted Proust in the Ritz in 1917. She lived at the hotel and offered him the sanctuary of her suite.

(*Right*) A table set in a private dining-room at the Ritz.

In those years, too, he began regular nocturnal visits to male brothels, mysterious and unrecorded errands probably of mixed motive, both for his own personal satisfaction and again field-work for the episodes of Charlus at Jupien's brothel. In fact he helped an old acquaintance, an ex-footman of the nobility, to open a male brothel at 11 rue de l'Arcade, even providing this Albert Le Cuziat with some of his parents' furniture, a gift prompted by kindness yet also by a secret pleasure of desecration. It is notable, though, that one of the reasons for befriending both the maître d'hôtel of the Ritz and the maître of this lesser establishment was to obtain information – Proust carefully and constantly pumped both of these reservoirs for their knowledge of social behaviour. Again a weather eye on his long main chance. But he was a man always of two opposite intentions – immensely self-centred, hugely magnanimous.

Paris was changed again. The motor-car had become as usual as the horse, the streets were coloured not only by the uniforms of the French Army but by those of the Allies, ending with a great influx

Paris was varied by many new and foreign uniforms, here seen in the Bois de Boulogne in June 1919. Proust was interested in this phenomenon.

L'Avenue du Bois, by Ernest Renoux, painted before the rich broke it up to build their new mansions. Proust regretted the move to this area from the Faubourg Saint-Germain where the pre-war Guermantes lived.

of Americans. Though fuel and light were harder to come by, building must have continued, so that the Prince de Guermantes could at the end of the war move to his new mansion on the Avenue du Bois. Fashions had become 'warlike'; women ran around in turbans, rings and bracelets were made of shell fragments. The lights at night were blacked out, but the play of searchlights scissored and sailed across a new kind of night-sky throbbing with enemy engines. The sunset was peopled by the 'brown gnats' of defending aircraft; on quiet nights, when the restaurants were closed and the traffic past, a moonlit Paris seemed strangely like the country, a night-scene the invalid could notice – for the ordinary daytime life was hearsay: Proust of the Ritz was now redoubling his work, conceiving the war chapter of *Time Regained*, transferring Tansonville and Combray from his child-hood Beauce to the front line near Rheims, receiving now the first bulk of new proofs of *Within a Budding Grove*, and getting together the material for his book of parodies and essays *Pastiches et mélanges*. These two books, and a new edition of *Swann's Way*, were finally published in June 1919.

96

Frontispiece of *L'Illustration* (1915).
It is called 'First night of Spring in
Paris', and shows a Zeppelin crossed
by searchlights. At the same time,
spirited Parisians were setting off
fireworks; witnesses regretted that
these did not explode the dirigible.
Proust was also a spirited Parisian,
and never feared a night-walk during
the raids.

(*Below*) A pause towards the Front
in 1914. Though insulated by illness
in Paris, Proust felt for these soldiers,
and for friends of his in uniform.

(*Left*) *Jean Cocteau*, by Jacques-Emile Blanche (1912). (*Right*) *Paul Valéry*, by the same painter (1913). Both Valéry and Cocteau were part of a new wave of writers with whom Proust was identified after the First World War.

(*Opposite*) The actress Réjane posed very correctly as the Prince de Sagan, a fashionable man-about-town who, aged and portly, suggested to Proust something of Baron de Charlus. Réjane harboured Proust in a flat in her house, until he took residence in the rue Hamelin (*below*) where eventually he was to die.

As peace came to Europe, Proust's personal race with death began its serious acceleration. One more unsolicited profit from the war came to him – flowering so late on the scene, he became associated with a new *cadre* of writers like Gide and Valéry and Cocteau, rather than the now *passé* Anatole France and Edmond Rostand of his earlier period. He had chosen well with the N.R.F.; now he applied for the Prix Goncourt.

However, just as in 1914 the death of Agostinelli had embittered the flavour of *Swann's Way*'s reception, so now a domestic catastrophe came to complicate the pleasure of his new publications: his aunt sold his home in the Boulevard Haussmann to a bank, he had to move. This was a matter of earthquake gravity: not only were both his private hospital ward and workshop disrupted, but he would now have to move out of the district sacred to his and his parents' lifetime.

He was still rich by some standards, but not his own; he felt he must be careful. In the event, his friend the Duc de Guiche arranged the cancellation of rental debts, others helped him with the sale of furniture, and he moved in May to a temporary haven in a furnished flat in the actress Réjane's house at No. 8 *bis* rue Laurent-Pichat. It proved too noisy; and after four months he took up residence in his final apartment on the fifth floor of a quiet and narrow street towards the Trocadéro, 44 rue Hamelin. Thus in comparatively smaller circumstances, he arranged the copper-coloured brass bedstead of his childhood against the wall and, with the little bamboo bedside-table piled with manuscript, went again to work and this time to await the Prix Goncourt result. In December the prize was awarded to him for *Within a Budding Grove*. The decision was not altogether popular. Several critics thought him too old for a prize which was intended for younger authors; others considered that it was a waste to present the prize-money to a man of such ample means. However, such controversy only gave greater publicity to the award – now Proust was famous throughout France, and he had obtained the large readership he had always desired.

In 1920 he received the Légion d'honneur, and, in October of that year, the first part of *The Guermantes Way* was published. In the following spring came the second part of *The Guermantes Way* and

MARCEL PROUST

A LA RECHERCHE
DU TEMPS PERDU.
TOME II

A L'OMBRE
DES JEUNES FILLES
EN FLEURS

nrf

PARIS
EDITIONS DE LA
NOUVELLE REVUE FRANÇAISE
35 ET 37, RUE MADAME, 1920

Within a Budding Grove, inscribed for Princess Soutzo (1920).

the first of *Sodome et Gomorrhe* (*Cities of the Plain*), whose essay on sodomy might earlier have proved dangerously shocking. But it was treated now as a moral treatise, and shocked only the inner camp of inverts, such as Gide, for its representation of homosexuality in a not too savoury way, illustrated by the ageing, such as Charlus, rather than by the young and beautiful. Proust had in fact transferred his own experience of homosexual love to romantic portrayals of young women in the novel (though his own romantic love of some women was always intermingled). What of himself an author puts into a book can never be surely judged, even if he himself confirms it, for he does not know what unconsciously he has done. Together with this question now came the discussion among Proust's friends and in society of the aspect of the novel as a *roman à clef*: Mme de Chevigné was displeased, and there was the danger that Montesquiou might recognize himself in Charlus. All such social and aesthetic perils had to be fenced with and fought at this time when he became iller and iller, more and more fearful of the immediacy of death, more and more pressed in the task of completing his still unfinished work.

View of Delft, by Jan Vermeer, which Proust saw in 1921 at an exhibition of Dutch paintings at the Jeu de Paume. The stillness of every golden summer's evening, of memory and Time, shines from this picture. Proust, giddy with illness himself at the time, wrote the experience into the death of Bergotte.

(*Below*) Photograph of Proust on the day he saw the *View of Delft*.

The apartment became barer as he got rid of unnecessary furniture; and now his young secretary for some years, Henri Rochat, the last of the silent captives, had to leave him. Very occasionally he still attended a ball or a *soirée*, and is reported as having a sort of ghostly youthfulness about him, the opposite to descriptions of the waxen effigy of the ill man when visited in bed. On one now memorable day he rose early and visited the loan exhibition of Dutch painting, suffering there a turn of giddiness, which he afterwards transmitted to a key passage describing the collapse of the writer Bergotte before Vermeer's *View of Delft*: death was again well in mind. In December, Montesquiou died, a further milestone: the great *poseur* still raved from the grave, frightening people with the barbed imminence of his posthumous memoirs; though they proved finally not so dangerous, drawing from the gracious Mme Greffulhe a remark to weight his tomb forever: 'It's not quite what one expects of a dead man.'

At this time Proust had also been manœuvring, like an astute man of business, the publication of long excerpts from the novel in literary magazines; with special revisions and cuttings and typings, this was all harder work than it sounds, and must have weighed heavily on these last years of prodigious effort. In 1922 he was at work on revisions of the next volumes, and *Cities of the Plain* II was published at the beginning of May. Then came an alarming accident – he swallowed undiluted adrenalin by mistake and his stomach felt seriously burned. He thought he had destroyed himself. He ordered ices and iced beer

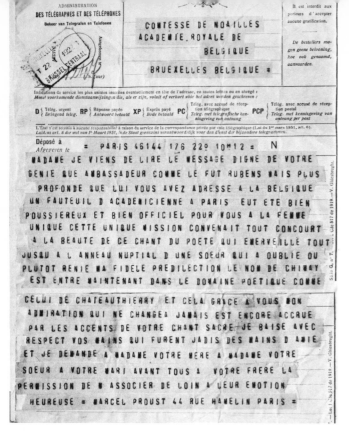

MADAME JE VIENS DE LIRE LE MESSAGE DIGNE DE VOTRE
GENIE QUE AMBASSADEUR COMME LE FUT RUBENS MAIS PLUS
PROFONDE QUE LUI VOUS AVEZ ADRESSE A LA BELGIQUE
UN FAUTEUIL D ACADEMICIENNE A PARIS EUT ETE BIEN
POUSSIEREUX ET BIEN OFFICIEL POUR VOUS A LA FEMME
UNIQUE CETTE UNIQUE MISSION CONVENAIT TOUT CONCOURT
A LA BEAUTE DE CE CHANT DU POETE QUI EMERVEILLE TOUT
JUSQU A L ANNEAU NUPTIAL D UNE SOEUR QUI A OUBLIE OU
PLUTOT RENIE MA FIDELE PREDILECTION LE NOM DE CHIMAY
EST ENTRE MAINTENANT DANS LE DOMAINE POETIQUE COMME
CELUI DE CHATEAUTHIERRY ET CELA GRACE A VOUS MON
ADMIRATION QUI NE CHANGEA JAMAIS EST ENCORE ACCRUE
PAR LES ACCENTS DE VOTRE CHANT SACRE JE BAISE AVEC
RESPECT VOS MAINS QUI FURENT JADIS DES MAINS D AMIE
ET JE DEMANDE A MADAME VOTRE MERE A MADAME VOTRE
SOEUR A VOTRE MARI AVANT TOUS A VOTRE FRERE LA
PERMISSION DE M ASSOCIER DE LOIN A LEUR EMOTION
HEUREUSE = MARCEL PROUST 44 RUE HAMELIN PARIS =

Twenty-line congratulatory telegram
to the Comtesse de Noailles when she
was received into the Belgian
Literary Academy (1922). Proust,
though ill and shortly to die, still
troubled to send his habitual long
and thoughtful telegrams.

*The Comtesse Anna de Noailles writing
in bed*, by Edouard Vuillard. Like
Proust, she wrote in bed.

The Abbé Arthur Mugnier, a courageous and saintly priest who helped many people of many kinds, including those of 'high' Society and those who had fallen 'low', and writers as various as Proust and Henry de Montherlant. For several years he held an anniversary service for Proust, until the time came when no one came. The pastel portrait is by the Comtesse Greffulhe.

for a month. It was a near-fatal strain on his debilitated organism. Yet that organism seemed to be fighting on his side too; the worrying symptoms of giddiness and the aphasic blurrings of speech disappeared. In July he went to a new restaurant, Le Bœuf sur le Toit, and, insulted by a drunk, went so far as to challenge him to a duel with swords! But the gesture was out of date, the affair amicably settled.

In September he was attacked most severely by his asthma, and suspected that cracks in the chimney were afflicting him with carbon monoxide poisoning. From then on he ordered that the fire should not be lit, dispensing with one of his greatest needs. In October the last *soirée* he ever went to, at Comte Etienne de Beaumont's, brought him down with a cold. Bronchitis and pneumonia followed, and on 18 November delirium and death. He had worked on until the middle of the night before, and his last spoken words, transcribed by the faithful Céleste, were of doctors and the death of Bergotte.

The dead Proust, etched by Paul
Helleu (1922).

Later, attending the dead body, Cocteau said of the piles of manuscript volumes on the mantelpiece that they were 'continuing to live,
like the ticking watch on the wrist of a dead soldier'.

The watch ticks on. And now we must try to discuss a little of what
is inside it. But it is a watch so great, like a whole new city to be discovered, that the visitor's impressions are bound to be largely subjec-
tive. My own stem first from what I feel are all-important words he
himself uses. Writing of the sensory experiences and intellectual
quests described at such refined length in the novel, he asserts that they
exist in every man: '. . . the life which, in a sense, dwells at every
instant in all men, and not the artist alone'. Quite. Otherwise few
readers would be able to understand or identify themselves with the
book. So it is not, as mistakenly is often supposed, a long treatise for
the aesthete; in spite of often painstaking demands on the reader, it
concerns itself with problems and questions and doubts which might
occur from time to time in the mind of any thinking man. In an aerial,
fabulous way it is down to earth.

Briefly – an absurd word in this context – the novel describes his
own experience of life, from childhood to middle age. It is not autobiographical, but experience condensed into fiction. All authors in
varying ways write from their own experience. Proust differed in
keeping very close to it, never deviating from his one obsessive problem: What is life about, what is all this I am seeing and feeling, and
why is it? Supremely sensitive, and with a prodigious memory for
recording sensations, he laid his own mind and body open like an
intricate musical instrument for experience to play on, studying every
note, always searching for a mysterious underlying theme half-
perceived from the first. This theme he was to discover as Time, not

as a passing essence but glassed in as a perpetual present by the extra-ordinary workings of human memory, willed or involuntary. Involuntary memory was the greatest proof: the way music, or a taste or touch, or any physical sensation can re-erect a scene of years ago in one phantasmal second. The senses thus were more important than the intellect. Yet it was the intellect which suggested to him that the final preservation of time, via the senses, was in the function of Art: moments of the past could be forever preserved in a book, a painting. Thus Vermeer's *View of Delft* preserves forever the magical fall of light and the painter's exaltation on the exact day long ago when it was painted. Thus, too, at the end of the great journey of *A la recherche*, the narrator decides to write a book recording his past: and, like the solid proof at the end of a conjuring trick, we suddenly find the book already written and in our hands. Here we are happy to observe that in fact the author Proust and the narrator Marcel part company. Unlike the dilettante and leisurely narrator, who discovers his ambition late in life, Proust the professional hard worker found it earlier and has already written the book.

First movement of Sonata for violin and piano, by Camille Saint-Saëns. This was possibly part of 'the little phrase' of Vinteuil.

In his quest into the mystery of Time, Proust is playing with magical convictions most people know: the pleasantly conceived certainty that all the past is golden, that the summers then were always sunny; and the mysterious suspicion that once there was a secret garden seen, and never again found; and the oddly satisfactory 'I-have-been-here-before' sensation of a place never visited previously; and the whole nostalgia of sound summed up in the phrase 'how potent cheap music is'; and the reawakening of uniquely pleasurable tastes whose simplest common denominator is Mum's Apple Pie. Thus we are all walking computers carrying about the records of past angles of light, sounds, tastes which, when by chance brought to our notice again, provoke a most mysterious and satisfying thrill: momentarily, we are outside Time. These are occasions when we are made abruptly conscious of traceable past sensations: but it is also probable that unconsciously the same thing is occurring all the time, that whenever we look at or feel a thing, the pleasure of memory lies beneath it. Human animals wish to survive and pain tends to be pushed out of the past, leaving the memory as a vehicle for happiness, pleasure, content. Proust concluded that this was the most important aspect of living, and devoted his life's work to its investigation and record.

Within this thematic framework, the long novel concerns itself with the evocation and passing of several decades of Parisian Society, of love-affairs, of people. People are never what you first think they are, they are changing all the time, their characters remain only broadly the same with many hidden and disparate facets always ready to reveal themselves. Love is not the unique and lasting bond you imagine, but a passing emotion best preserved in memory and even best enjoyed as an unrequited passion, in the absence of the beloved. Society appears glamorous, elegant, intelligent, but is discovered to be snobbish, cruel, fatuous, and fated like everything else to change, grow old and die with the passage of time. In every sphere of life enchantment, in fact, becomes disenchantment. Only the memory, and the memory embalmed in art, escapes.

To penetrate the years and illustrate these themes, Proust introduces us to a most visible world of varying places peopled by characters who are always of interest because all the time they are changing, forever about to spring a surprise on us. Thus the memorable Baron de Charlus is met first as a fashionable nobleman with some unstated aura of mystery behind an arrogant façade: only many volumes later is he revealed as a homosexual; and while his wild arrogance makes him a vehicle for some of the most hilarious passages in the book, and his last years in a wheel chair trying to seduce children are pathetic and horrible, nevertheless he is found to be generous and to have a kind heart. (In fact, while seeming to undress the secrets of his characters

(*Opposite*) Luncheon in the country. Proust is the third standing person from the left.

A kind of *salon* given by *arrivistes* such as Proust's character Mme Verdurin.

without mercy, Proust makes at one point a sudden and most merciful genuflection to the human herd instinct: 'It is not common sense which is the most widespread thing in the world, it is kindness.') With another main character, Mme Verdurin, we find first a pretentious *arriviste* holding a bourgeois and arch *salon*, a figure of some ridicule throughout the book, yet also capable of an act of sudden generosity; and she it is who somersaults the whole social fabric by becoming in the end, through a clever marriage, the most superior hostess of the Faubourg Saint-Germain. So it is with others, characters constantly changing character, from the rough intellectual writer Bloch smoothly conforming as he grows older and successful, to the heroic golden-haired officer-figure of faultless Saint-Loup who in the end deceives his wife openly with other women to hide his real propensity for young men.

To begin this vast canvas Proust plunges, in his first volumes, into the most evocative picture of a country childhood ever written. Heady with the smells of long-lost flowers, touching with the affections of family life in a slow country town, he evokes everybody's dream of sunny childhood days – the past we think we have had even if we only conceived it from long-ago pictures, books. The exact sensuous detail is astonishingly complete, from all the Maytime burgeoning of the

country around to the 'little patch of neglected earth' in his aunt's small garden, a dusty symbol of hours which nevertheless can hang heavy. The family is accustomed to take those two particular walks which haunt the boy's memory forever. One is the Méséglise way, up that little path bordered by pink-flowering hawthorn – the way that leads past the park of Swann's mansion of Tansonville with its lovely dress of lilacs, and is the way of love and innocence. Through a gap in the hawthorn hedge the boy sees, as in a secret garden, the pinafored little girl Gilberte with her pink freckles. It is a held moment of his first love. And it is curiously heightened by an indelicate gesture from the little girl.

For the way of the hawthorn path is never altogether innocent. It is in this direction that one day the boy spies on the window of a country house and sees there a scene of lesbian seduction, together with an episode of mental cruelty. He is learning. Here and there among the summer scents the paradise already shows symptoms of its coming loss. Proust is too inquiring to paint a saccharine summer without showing its darker implications.

The other walk he took was the way by the river, a different world of water-plants and violets, the more mysterious osiered way leading to the gloriously aristocratic château of Guermantes which he never

In his novel, Proust's narrator took boyhood walks towards an aristocratic château which he never then reached. In Proust's life, the château lay in the direction of Saint-Eman. For the novel, he borrowed the name 'Guermantes' for this ideal. Pictured here is the real Château de Guermantes, which happens to be centred with a clock, so that Time is reflected in the lake.

(*Left*) Liane de Pougy (Anne de Chassaigne), by Paul Berthon. She was one of the actress-whores of those times, called *les Orpingtons*, after the breed of *poules* called 'Buff Orpingtons'.

(*Right*) A daughter of Jethro, detail of a painting by Botticelli (*c.* 1481). In the novel, Charles Swann found her very like his love, Odette de Crécy.

reached, a dream remaining a dream, like the rivery hope of a source. They passed big-eyed childhood interests – a mysterious angler, lonely women in summer-houses – and sometimes returned by early moonlight when a poetic white luminescence broke the town's known buildings into a new and enthralling beauty. Thus the Guermantes way was the way of sophistication and dreams of worldly magnificence. Both these walks are intended symbols of life to come; as always with childhood walks they seem absolutely separate – only returning in middle age does the narrator find that their ends are not far distant, just as simple love and the complexities of society are intermingled. He finds the enchanting river of Merovingian dreams is only a dull stream, the source a boring bubble.

Directly after this immense description of a childhood paradise with its distant storm-clouds, the novelist describes at length a real storm in the removed world of grown-ups – a flashback in time to an old love-affair between Swann the owner of Tansonville and the cocotte Odette de Crécy. It occurred just before the time the narrator was born, a period so near yet so forever far, just missed, holding that special kind of unattainable nostalgia tinged with envy of one's parents for living then. The love-affair is racked with passionate troubles and jealousy, and shadows a prevision of what the narrator himself will suffer in days to come.

The civilized and gentlemanly Swann hovers like a dark angel in the novel. He is the one whose evening visits steal the young narrator's mother's interest, so that she denies the boy his longed-for good-night kiss, the key moment never forgotten. Swann is the sound of other people enjoying themselves on a summer's evening when the boy is in bed. Swann is also the father of Gilberte, with whom soon the young Marcel is to fall in love when he meets her again in the Champs-Elysées gardens in Paris. And it is Swann's whole household which holds much more glamour for the boy than his own home.

At the end of *Swann's Way*, we are jolted by a sudden flash forward to the present, when in middle age the narrator revisits the Bois de Boulogne where he once went to watch, in the fashionable Allée des Acacias, the elegant and lovely figure of Mme Swann. Then was a

L'Allée des Acacias, drawn for *Le Rire* by Capiello, showing particularly the actress Polaire in the centre, as well as others, like Sorel and Réjane. An elegant type of traffic jam; but it was usually more leisurely, for this is a visual joke.

Times and fashion were changing, and so were the movements of women. Here Sabattier illustrates the fairly new *montre-bracelet* (1921).

(*Right*) An earlier gesture of the nostalgic past by Paul Helleu (*c.* 1906).

golden time of delight, 'a time when I still had faith'. Now it is all changed. The fashions look incongruous, motor-cars have replaced the glittering equipages of horse and carriage. Time has stolen the old reality; his saddened last words are: '. . . remembrance of a particular form is but regret for a particular moment; and houses, roads, avenues are as fugitive, alas, as the years'.

We feel that here perhaps is a complete novel. Possibly it was originally so intended. Yet if so, its inspiration irritated the author into producing the pearls of ten further volumes, and a final solution to his lifelong quandary, quest, yearning. That yearning is singularly well expressed in the next two books, *Within a Budding Grove*, which largely deal with impressions of adolescence and finally Marcel's visit to the Normandy seaside where he becomes obsessed with a happy extrovert band of girls seen passing on the promenade. He, the lonely introvert, longs for their easy frivolity. Finally he meets them, becomes accepted, settles his attention – not quite love – on the one called Albertine. By now he has already experienced the decline of love with

Gilberte Swann. He has experienced other disillusionments: with the seaside town of Balbec he had looked forward to a romantically rocky and stormy northern coast, but found only a neatly villa-ed resort; and visiting the theatre in Paris he had been wildly excited before seeing the great actress Berma (a Sarah Bernhardt, although the name recalls that there was at the time an actress called La Brema) yet had been disappointed by her reality. We are introduced to the further theme that anticipation is sweeter than possession.

Meanwhile, he has met the writer Bergotte and the painter Elstir, whose personalities do not match their work, but whose work at least does not disillusion him. Also, in the earlier Swann story, the narrator has felt the appeal of the composer Vinteuil. Art is already seen to survive life's usual letdowns. To this may be added private ecstasies in line with the original madeleine soaked in lime-tea: notably now the sight, on a drive in the country near Hudimesnil, of three trees which excite him mysteriously, but whose strange power he cannot analyse beyond feeling that, though it is impossible, he has known

Sarah Bernhardt in *Ruy Blas*, at the time the young Proust went first to the theatre; from this experience came the character he called 'Berma'.

(*Right*) A contemporary actress, Marie Brema, playing Dalila in *Samson et Dalila*.

(*Left*) César Franck, the composer who probably contributed to the character Vinteuil.

(*Right*) Camille Barrère, a diplomat who may well have suggested various attributes for the character Norpois.

them before. Such close observations of interior feelings are just as important as his impressions of the real world, and form part of a truly deep picture of the adolescence of a precocious youth who can fall in love, criticize art, observe grown-up behaviour with meticulous accuracy, get drunk, yet cry himself to sleep when his grandmother forgets to kiss him good-night.

On the way now many of the main characters of the novel have been met; the diplomat Norpois, Cottard the doctor, the Baron de Charlus, Saint-Loup, the Marquise de Villeparisis, Albertine and others who will all reappear throughout the long tale of time to come, each affecting the other in a thousand subtle ways, living in some sort of hall of echoes, dancing a slow saraband of mirrors, until the final moment when time is regained by the most persistent of narrators. It would plainly be ridiculous here to attempt to compress the whole story of these twelve volumes. One can only reflect a general impression, investigate a few techniques. How, for instance, *The Guermantes Way* brings a dazzling picture of *fin de siècle salons* and Society, and describes a new and unrequited love of the narrator for a great, fashionable social figure, the glamorous and extraordinary bird-faced

Duchesse de Guermantes. In this and later descriptions of the palmy and plush echelons of High Society, it is extraordinary how Proust can with such enthusiasm describe their sensuous colour and glitter, while at the same time slowly revealing how empty, snobbish and corrupt they really are. It is sometimes with sharply impassive wit that he manages this, for instance describing the aristocrats in their boxes during the jewelled description of the Opéra-Comique audience – how they sit in so many little drawing-rooms, resting indifferent hands on gilded columns, making it seem 'that they and they only would have had minds free to listen to the play, if only they had had minds'. But the essence of this otherwise long description of the immense coral plush theatre is to enframe the white swansdown elegance of the two boxed goddesses, the Duchesse and Princesse de Guermantes, and the whole evocation remains one of the great set-pieces by which readers most remember the novel. Submerged in such a labyrinth of twelve volumes, dazed by the intricate interplay of characters, it is natural enough that such moments of clear illumination or action stay the more fixed in memory. It may be for some the great glassy seaside restaurant of Rivebelle, where Marcel dines intoxicatedly with Saint-

Le Pré Catelan, a fashionable restaurant, painted by Henri Gervex (1909). Situated in the Bois de Boulogne, it has much of the glassy and watery character of Proust's seaside Rivebelle.

Les Belles de nuit au jardin de Paris, by Jean Béraud (1905). Such were the pleasures of the French summer.

Loup in a room where the waiters fly about like birds and the assemblage of round white tables seems like an astral harmony of planets. Others may remember most the many and distressing pages recording the slow death of Marcel's beloved grandmother, where different doctors engrossed in their own obsessive theories diagnose wrongly, where the old woman slowly disintegrates with pain and morphine, blindness and deafness, where at one moment she who was disgusted by them submitted to leeches – 'fastened to her neck, her temples, her ears, the tiny black serpents were writhing among her bloodstained locks, as on the head of Medusa'. Then, in a very different vein, one recalls easily many hilarious scenes with the Baron de Charlus, particularly when he rages so unpredictably and so high and for so long at the narrator that this latter, passive and innocent, suddenly picks up the Baron's tall hat and stamps on it – whereon the eccentric nobleman coolly calls for another to replace it. Or it may be less a scene than one or other of the arrogant workings of the Baron's extraordinary mind – like his opinion on the large socio-political issue of the Dreyfus Case, that Dreyfus cannot be a traitor since he is not a Frenchman but a Jew. Or exact descriptions of his homosexual glare, the glaucous stare, the shifting eye, the defensive trumpetings against effeminacy in young men.

Such memorable issues of poetic reality seem to stand out because of Proust's technique. Throughout the work he interrupts action with long disquisitions on any matter to hand, the nature of time or art, the nautical life of Renaissance Venice, the science of military strategy, the various kinds of jealousy stimulating a love-affair, the parallel between the exclusion of inverts and of Jews. At first these long interruptions may irritate, may seem like self-indulgence on the author's part, until one realizes that they are all part of the narrator's mind and therefore legitimate, for a person cannot exist without a mind, thought, opinions, internal questionings. Altogether it feels less like reading the work of a novelist than that of some supreme psychological scientist who is also a Sunday painter: painting may come more quickly to mind than poetry, because of Proust's strong visual and tactile senses, and of his insistent use of metaphor and visual simile. A passing example of this: speaking of the lavatory in the Champs-Elysées, 'those cubicles of stone in which men crouch like sphinxes'. Exact. Or another example more in line with the usual sinuous length

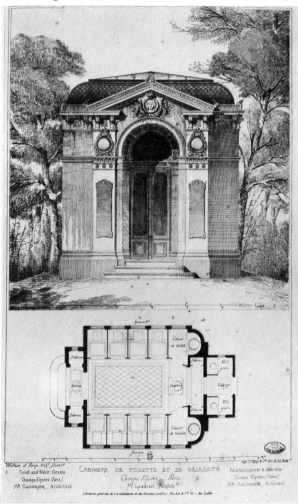

Elevation and plan for a civil architecture in the Champs-Elysées by Gaudrier (c. 1865). Proust uses this curious setting in a symbolic way to illustrate the vanity of Society, comparing the attendant and her regular 'clients' to Mme Verdurin and her little circle. Critical passages in the novel occur in such *cabinets de nécéssite*; in the plan one may see '. . . those cubicles of stone in which men crouch like sphinxes' (*Within a Budding Grove* I).

of his sentences, part, and only part, of an involved appreciation of a table after dining:

Since I had seen such things depicted in water-colours by Elstir, I sought to find again in reality, I cherished, as though for their poetic beauty, the broken gestures of the knives still lying across one another, the swollen convexity of a discarded napkin upon which the sun would patch a scrap of yellow velvet, the half-empty glass which thus shewed to greater advantage the noble sweep of its sides . . . the shifting colour of the plums which passed from green to blue and from blue to golden yellow in the half-plundered dish, the chairs, like a group of old ladies, that came twice daily to take their places round the white cloth spread on the table as on an altar . . . where in the hollows of oyster-shells a few drops of lustral water had gathered as in tiny holy water stoups of stone; I tried to find beauty there *where I had never imagined before that it could exist,* in the most ordinary things, in the profundities of 'still life' [my italics].

Long passages of introspection arrest the life of the characters. Although at one moment intensely real, they are suddenly stopped in full motion, and feel to the reader to be held in suspense like the life-size figures of a fresco: like the Mantegna figures at Mantua, like the fully dressed garden-party figures of the Belgian painter Delvaux, like the adolescent dreamers of Balthus. Turn the pages, and they are kicked back to life. But for long moments they stand and wait, embalmed in time. Time is played with in the whole construction, with its flashbacks and flashforwards, its sudden jumps over the years: one day can take 287 pages, yet years can pass unrecorded. This is, of course, intentional. Some of the narrative, however, can be questioned: for instance, Swann's old love-affair – how could anyone from hearsay retell a story in such intimate detail? The account can seem to be an impossible fiction within a probable fiction, endangering the suspension of disbelief.

Proust's literary influences were many, he was an omnivorous reader: some of the most apparent sources include the sinuous intrigue of Saint-Simon's memoirs, the painterly vision of Ruskin, the feeling for time past in Chateaubriand, Baudelaire, Nerval. Painting and music were of equal influence, the canvases of Monet and Helleu, the compositions of César Franck and Saint-Saëns. But the overriding influence was the all-important seed of his own life. Lifting one's eyes from such omniscience, it is extraordinary to reflect how blind Proust could at times be to himself. He could criticize Robert de Billy for using 'too many adjectives'. He could expatiate: 'A book in which there are theories is like an article from which the price tag has not been removed' – that from the most explicit of writers! And of Rémy de Gourmont's assertion: 'One writes well only about the things one hasn't lived through', he is able to declare, 'That is my whole work.' He objects to novels in which the author is always getting characters into their overcoats – replace 'overcoats' with 'cabs' and you have Proust himself.

But these are minor pinpricks which will do little to deflate the huge dirigible. Proust is one of the few literary geniuses of the twentieth century, and when his long book comes to a climax with a telling new onrush of involuntary memories followed by the astonishing *danse macabre* of social characters now under a snowfall of white hair at the last reception of the new Princesse de Guermantes – we feel that indeed his quest was worth while, his search for lost time fulfilled, and that on the way all our lives have been illuminated. We remember the ordinary household sounds that inspired his memory, the singing of water-pipes, the coughing of central heating; smells like that of kindling wood in a hearth; or the sensory touch of a starched napkin: and we may wonder whether in the future there will be equally treasurable sensations recalled from the dross of our present time, the whine of a vacuum-cleaner, the belling of ice-cream vans, the thunder of jet aircraft, the little smell of a boiling tin label, the dead touch of plastic surfaces, the dunking of a doughnut in instant coffee . . . and wonder too where our own experience has been touched before by some of his evocations, for instance that major mythical mother-figure standing by the bedside in evening dress – a good-night kiss, it would not be *lèse majesté* to suggest, from Mrs Darling in *Peter Pan*?

In the first sentence of the novel the word 'time' has appeared. Thereafter throughout the volumes it is reiterated, sung sometimes softly, sometimes drummed loud, but always there, until, in the very last sentence, this quintessence of the book receives the accolade of a last word:

But at least, if strength were granted me for long enough to accomplish my work, I should not fail, even if the result was to make them resemble monsters, to describe men first and foremost as occupying a place, a very considerable place compared with the restricted one which is allotted to them in space, a place on the contrary immoderately prolonged – for simultaneously, like giants plunged into the years, they touch epochs that are immensely far apart, separated by the slow accretion of many, many days – in the dimension of Time.

CHRONOLOGY

1871 Marcel Proust born on 10 July.

1873 Robert Proust, his brother, born.

1880 First attack of asthma.

1882–89 Schooling at Lycée Condorcet. By 1886 has met Marie Bénardaky, his youthful love. Writes for school magazines. Attends the *salons* of Mmes Straus, Baignères, Lemaire.

1889 In November joins 76th Infantry Regiment at Orléans for one year's service.

1890 Grandmother, Mme Nathé Weil, dies in January. In November he enrolls as law student at the Sorbonne. In time a student of Bergson.

1892 Published in *Le Banquet*.

1893 Meets Comte Robert de Montesquiou, who introduces him into the highest Society. Published in *La Revue blanche*. In October, his degree in law.

1894 In May, attends Montesquiou's fête for Léon Delafosse.

1895 In March, his degree in philosophy. Joins the staff of the Mazarine Library, a sinecure which continues until 1900. During this and the preceding years, is active in Society, and travels abroad in Holland, Belgium, Germany and Switzerland.

1896 Great-uncle, Louis Weil, dies. His first book, *Les Plaisirs et les jours* is published in June. A start has been made on *Jean Santeuil*.

1897 Duel with Jean Lorrain.

1898 Collects signatures for a petition for revision of the Dreyfus Case.

1900 Publishes first articles on Ruskin. In May travels to Venice and Padua. The Proust family moves house to 45 rue de Courcelles.

1902 Visits Belgium and Holland in October.

1903 His brother, Dr Robert Proust, married. Excerpts from the translation of *The Bible of Amiens* published. In November, his father dies.

1904 *The Bible of Amiens* translation published.

1905 In September, his mother dies. In December, enters Dr Sollier's nursing-home for nervous disorders.

1906 In January, leaves nursing-home. Translation of *Sesame and Lilies* published. Spends August until December at Versailles, previous to moving in at 102 Boulevard Haussmann.

1907 Holiday at Cabourg, where he first meets Alfred Agostinelli and employs him as chauffeur.

1908 Spirited parodies based on the Lemoine Case published. Tells Mme Straus that he intends starting on a long work.

1909 Asks Georges de Lauris whether the name Guermantes would be free for use in a novel. Tells Mme Straus, in August, that he has just begun and finished a long book. This would refer to a first version of *A la recherche*.

1910 Cork lining installed in bedroom while he is at Cabourg.

1912 First version of *A la recherche* revised and typed. Agostinelli becomes resident secretary. *Le Figaro* publishes excerpts from the novel. The novel rejected by the N.R.F. and Fasquelle.

1913 The novel rejected by Ollendorff. In March it is accepted by Grasset, with Proust paying costs, and on 14 November *Du côté de chez Swann* is published.

1914 Death of Agostinelli in May. In June and July excerpts from *Le côté de Guermantes* published in the N.R.F.

1915 A summary of the Albertine story given to Mme Scheikévitch in November.

1916 Moves from Grasset to the N.R.F. as publisher.

1919 Has to leave the Boulevard Haussmann, stays for some months in Réjane's house before removal to 44 rue Hamelin.
A l'ombre des jeunes filles en fleurs published.
Pastiches et mélanges published.
Du côté de chez Swann reissued.
In December, *A l'ombre des jeunes filles en fleurs* is awarded the Prix Goncourt.

1920 Awarded the Légion d'honneur. *Le côté de Guermantes* I published.

1921 *Le côté de Guermantes* II and *Sodome et Gomorrhe* I published. Death of Montesquiou.

1922 *Sodome et Gomorrhe* II published. On 18 November, Proust dies.

1923 *La Prisonnière* published.

1925 *Albertine disparue* published.

1927 *Le Temps retrouvé* published.

SOME SOURCES OF PROUST'S CHARACTERS

(It must be remembered that, while Proust admitted taking some details from the habits and appearances of real people, he insisted that each character was finally fictitious, the amalgam of eight or ten or more observed prototypes.)

ALBERTINE   Alfred Agostinelli; Louisa de Mornand; Marie Finaly; Henri Rochat.

BERGOTTE   Anatole France; Marie-Alphonse Darlu; Alphonse Daudet; Ernest Renan; Proust himself.

BERMA   Sarah Bernhardt; Réjane.

BARON DE CHARLUS   Baron Doasan; Comte Robert de Montesquiou; Jean Lorrain.

ELSTIR   Monet; Helleu; Moreau; Whistler.

FRANÇOISE   Céleste Albaret; other servants like Céline, Félicie, and Ernestine of Illiers.

GILBERTE   Marie de Bénardaky; Jeanne Pouquet.

DUCHESSE DE GUERMANTES   Comtesse de Chevigné; Comtesse Greffulhe; Mme Straus.

PRINCESSE DE GUERMANTES   Comtesse Greffulhe.

JUPIEN   Albert Le Cuziat.

MOREL   Léon Delafosse; Henri Rochat.

ODETTE   Laure Hayman; the courtesan Léonie Closmesnil.

RACHEL   Louisa de Mornand; the courtesan Emilienne d'Alençon.

SAINT-LOUP   Comte Bertrand de Fénelon; Gaston Arman de Caillavet; Comte Gabriel de La Rochefoucauld; Comte Georges de Lauris.

SWANN   Charles Haas; Paul Hervieu; Emile Straus; Charles Ephrussi, Editor of the *Gazette des Beaux-Arts*; Proust himself.

MME VERDURIN   Mme Aubernon; Mme Arman de Caillavet; Mme Lemaire.

MARQUISE DE VILLEPARISIS   Comtesse de Beaulaincourt; Mme Lemaire.

VINTEUIL   César Franck; Debussy; Saint-Saëns.

A la recherche du temps perdu	English titles
Du côté de chez Swann	Swann's Way
A l'ombre des jeunes filles en fleurs	Within a Budding Grove
Le côté de Guermantes	The Guermantes Way
Sodome et Gomorrhe	Cities of the Plain
La Prisonnière	The Captive
Albertine disparue	The Sweet Cheat Gone
	(The above were all translated by C. K. Scott-Moncrieff.)
Le Temps retrouvé	Time Regained

(First translation by Stephen Hudson. Susequently published (1969) in a new translation by Andreas Mayor.)

LIST OF ILLUSTRATIONS

33 The house of the Amiot family. Photo Roger-Viollet

34 The garden of the Amiot family. Photo Roger-Viollet

35 *Little Girl with a Watering-Can*; painting by Auguste Renoir, 1876. National Gallery of Art, Washington, D.C., Chester Dale Collection

36 *Plage à Trouville*; painting by Claude Monet, c. 1870
Le Déjeuner; painting by Claude Monet, c. 1873. Musée du Louvre. Photo Giraudon

37 *Henriette in the Big Hat*; painting by Henri Evenepoel, 1899. Musées Royaux des Beaux-Arts, Brussels

38 Marcel Proust at the Lycée Condorcet; detail of photograph, c. 1887; Mante-Proust Collection
The Exit of the Lycée Condorcet; painting by Jean Béraud, 1903. Musée Carnavalet. Photo Giraudon

39 *The Moriss column*; painting by Jean Béraud. Musée Carnavalet. Photo Bulloz

40 The Statue of Liberty under construction in the yard of its designer, F. Bartholdi; painting by Victor Dargaud, 1883. Musée Carnavalet. Photo Giraudon

41 *L'Arc de Triomphe*; painting by Giuseppe De Nittis (1846–84). Courtesy of Messrs Sotheby
Mme Emile Straus, *née* Geneviève Halévy; painting by Elie Delaunay, 1878. Musée du Louvre. Photo Eileen Tweedy

42 *Anatole France*; etching by Edgar Chahine. Mansell Collection
Henri Bergson; painting by Jacques-Emile Blanche (1861–1942).

Musée des Beaux-Arts, Rouen. Photo Giraudon

43 Marcel Proust in uniform at the time of his military service in 1890, with inscription to Gaston Arman de Caillavet; Mante-Proust Collection

44 View of Cabourg-sur-Mer; photograph by Delahaye, c. 1900. Georges Sirot Collection

45 *Laure Hayman*; pastel by J.L. Stewart, 1882. Courtesy of Jean Dieterle. Photo Eileen Tweedy

46 *La Loge*; painting by Henri Gervex, c. 1880. Courtesy of Ferrers Gallery, London
The Comtesse Greffulhe, *née* Elisabeth de Caraman-Chimay; painting by Philip de László de Lombos, 1909. Courtesy of the Duc de Gramont. Photo Eileen Tweedy

47 Mme Straus surrounded by friends (Charles Haas on the left, Edgar Degas behind her); Mante-Proust Collection

48 Madeleine Lemaire in her studio; photograph by Nadar; Georges Sirot Collection
Mme de Barbarin (*née* Marie Finaly), and daughter. Courtesy Mme René Le Bret

49 Robert de Montesquiou-Fézensac, outside Le Pavillon des Muses, his house in the Boulevard Maillot, c. 1904. Bibliothèque Nationale

51 *The Interior of a pâtisserie*; painting by Jean Béraud, 1889. Musée Carnavalet. Photo Bulloz

52 *The Rue Royale Club in 1867*; from left to right Comte A. de la Tour-Maubourg, Marquis du Lau, Comte Etienne de Ganay, Comte Jean de Rochechouart, C. Van-

sittart, Marquis de Miramon, Baron Hottinguer, Marquis de Ganay, Gaston de Saint-Maurice, Prince de Polignac, Marquis de Gallifet, Charles Haas; painting by James Tissot, 1868. Photo Roger-Viollet

53 Madeleine Lemaire's Château de Réveillon (Seine-et-Marne), with inscription by her daughter; postcard; Mante-Proust Collection

54 The Comtesse Adhéaume de Chevigné, 1889. Bibliothèque Nationale
Batwing frock by Paul Poiret, with painted design by Mariano Fortuny, c. 1910. Collection de l'Union française des Arts du Costume. Photo Eileen Tweedy

55 *The Comtesse Anna de Noailles*; unfinished plaster bust by Auguste Rodin, c. 1906. Musée Rodin, Paris
Library of Princesse Mathilde at her country-house Saint-Gratien; painting by Charles Giraud. Courtesy of Pierre Fabius

56 A Society reception, c. 1890; Georges Sirot Collection

57 Reynaldo Hahn at home. Photo Roger-Viollet

58 Standing: Prince Edmond de Polignac, Princesse de Brancovan, Marcel Proust, Prince C. de Brancovan, Léon Delafosse. Second row: Mme de Montgenard, Princesse de Polignac, Comtesse Mathieu de Noailles. Front row: Princesse de Caraman-Chimay, Abel Hermant. Mante-Proust Collection
Poster for Katabexine, a remedy against coughs and asthma, designed by L. Cappiello

59 Poster for *La Revue blanche*, 1895, designed by H. Toulouse-Lautrec.

91 Reynaldo Hahn at the Western Front in the First World War. Mante-Proust Collection
Dr Robert Proust on leave in Paris during the First World War. Mante-Proust Collection

92 Christmas menu and cover, Ritz Hotel. Courtesy of Ritz Hotel, Paris

93 The Ritz Hotel, Paris. Courtesy of Ritz Hotel, Paris.

94 *The Princesse Soutzo* (later Mme Paul Morand); painting by Lucien Lévy-Dhurmer. Courtesy of M. and Mme Paul Morand. Photo Eileen Tweedy
A private dining-room at the Ritz Hotel. Courtesy of Ritz Hotel, Paris

95 A morning in the Bois de Boulogne; after J. Simont, from *L'Illustration*, 7 June 1919. British Museum

96 *Avenue du Bois*; painting by Ernest Renoux (1863–1932). Courtesy of the Kaplan Gallery, London

97 Zeppelin caught in searchlights; frontispiece of *L'Illustration*, 27 March 1915. British Museum
Soldiers at a station, 1914; Georges Sirot Collection

98 *Jean Cocteau*; painting by Jacques-Emile Blanche, 1912. Musée des Beaux-Arts, Rouen. Photo Giraudon
Paul Valéry; painting by Jacques-Emile Blanche, 1913. Musée des Beaux-Arts, Rouen. Photo Giraudon

99 Réjane as the Prince de Sagan, inscribed to Marcel Proust. Georges Sirot Collection
The rue Hamelin; postcard. Bibliothèque historique de la ville de Paris

100 Title page of *A l'ombre des jeunes filles en fleurs*; N.R.F. edition, 1920, with a letter to Princesse Soutzo. Courtesy of M. and Mme Paul Morand

101 *View of Delft*; painting by Jan Vermeer. Mauritshuis, The Hague
Marcel Proust, on leaving the exhibition of Dutch paintings at the Jeu de Paume, May 1921

102 Telegram to the Comtesse de Noailles, 22 January 1922. Courtesy Comte Anne-Jules de Noailles
The Comtesse Anna de Noailles writing in bed; painting by Edouard Vuillard. Private Collection

103 The Abbé Arthur Mugnier, pastel by the Comtesse Greffulhe. Princesse Bibesco Collection. Photo Connaissance des Arts

104 Proust on his death-bed; etching by Paul Helleu, 1922

105 First movement of Sonata for violin and piano, by Camille Saint-Saëns. Bibliothèque Nationale

107 Marcel Proust among his relations at lunch in the open air. Mante-Proust Collection

108 Musical entertainment in a Paris *salon*; cartoon from *Le Rire*, 24 December 1898. British Museum

109 Château de Guermantes, near Lagny. Photo Giraudon

110 Poster for the Folies-Bergère with Liane de Pougy; design by Paul Berthon. Photo Messrs Christie, London
Detail from *Moses and the Daughters of Jethro*; fresco by Sandro Botticelli, 1481–83. Sistine Chapel, Rome. Photo Anderson

111 L'Allée des Acacias; illustration by L. Capiello from *Le Rire*, 24 June 1899. British Museum

112 A new gesture; illustration by L. Sabattier from *L'Illustration*, 17 November 1921

113 *La Robe relevée*; etching by P. Helleu, c. 1906. Courtesy of *Editions Graphiques*, London

113 Sarah Bernhardt in *Ruy Blas* by Victor Hugo; painting by G. Clairin. Comédie-Française, Paris. Photo Giraudon
Mme Brema as Dalila; illustration from *Théâtre*. Bibliothèque de l'Arsenal, Paris

114 César Franck. Georges Sirot Collection
Camille Barrère. Photo by Pirou. Georges Sirot Collection

115 *Le Pré Catelan*; painting by Henri Gervex, 1909. Courtesy Gérard Seligmann. Photo Eileen Tweedy

116 *Les Belles de nuit au jardin de Paris*; painting by Jean Béraud, 1905. Photo Bulloz

117 Design for a public lavatory in the Champs-Elysées by the architect Gaudrier, c. 1865. Bibliothèque Nationale

BIBLIOGRAPHICAL NOTE

The great list of books about Proust is surely headed by George D. Painter's finely documented two-volume work, *Marcel Proust. A Biography* (London and Boston, 1959, 1965). Mr Painter has also translated and edited a collection of Proust's letters, *Marcel Proust, Letters to his Mother* (London 1956, New York 1957). A useful general selection of further letters in English translation is by Mina Curtiss, *Letters of Marcel Proust* (New York 1949, London 1950). Further reading might include, among much else, *The Magic Lantern of Marcel Proust* by Howard Moss (London and New York 1962), *Marcel Proust. Documents iconographiques* by Georges Cattaui (Geneva 1956), *The Two Worlds of Marcel Proust* by Harold March (Oxford 1948, New York 2nd ed. 1961), *Marcel Proust* by Richard H. Barker (New York 1958, London 1959), and *A la recherche de Marcel Proust* by André Maurois (Paris 1949).

INDEX

Entries in parenthesis refer to places and characters in *Remembrance of Things Past*; figures in italic refer to illustrations

DATE DUE